American Indian Mythology

Top and side views of bowl with fertility designs.

American Indian Mythology

ALICE MARRIOTT AND CAROL K. RACHLIN

THOMAS Y. CROWELL COMPANY · ESTABLISHED 1834 · NEW YORK

Designed by Susan Gibson

Manufactured in the United States of America

ISBN 0-690-07201-5

6   7   8   9   10

FOR

Ben Rachlín and Sydney C. Marriott

WHO MADE IT POSSIBLE

ACKNOWLEDGMENTS

Our gratitudes are many. To Junius Bird and Philip Gifford of the American Museum of Natural History, to Robert Bell and James Bragg of the University of Oklahoma, and to Dr. and Mrs. Harry L. Deupree of Oklahoma City for photographic material. To the Parker family for the portrait of Quanah and his friend Quessyah. To our friends the informants and interpreters, named and unnamed, who brought this book about. And, finally, to the lady with the bullwhip, our personal Grandmother Spider, Nannine Joseph.

CONTENTS

ix

Part Three: THE WORLD WE LIVE IN NOW

Part Four: THE WORLD WE GO TO

PHOTOGRAPHS

Frontispiece. Bowl with fertility designs

[Following page 62]

War dancers at powwow
Cooking food for powwow
Young dancer in full headdress
Old Kiowa man
Quanah Parker and friend
Peyote ritual equipment
Kiowa peyote fan

[Following page 140]

Rain god from Tesuque Pueblo
Painted rain god from Tesuque Pueblo
Hopi rabbit kachina
Hopi-carved "Navaho" tablita kachina
Ojibway beaded cuff
Ponca beaded purse
Cheyenne pipe and pipe bag
Man's beaded dance apron
Water jar from Laguna Pueblo
Bowl from Sitkyatki Site

American Indian Mythology

Introduction: Four World Corners

In the closely twined cord of any people's lore and religion and history, there must be ravelings as well as knots. Often it is difficult to tease out the end to which a frayed strand leads.

The folklorist can never cease to be aware of this basic problem. Somehow, he must find the means to disentangle belief from fact, and to check his facts—once separated—against the lore that has been gathered and recorded from other peoples in other parts of the world.

For the anthropologist-folklorist, the demands of scientific conscience and of accuracy are perhaps more stringent than those made on the more casual collector of folk customs and folk tales. It is the bounden duty of the anthropologist to know first the history, as distinguished from the lore, of a given culture. Then he must learn that group's own interpretation of our common history, before he crosses the boundaries separating fact from legend from myth.

In this book the compilers, both anthropologists rather than folklorists, are attempting to present as best they can the lore of a people whose ways and customs are steadily combining with our own. "Myth" as we shall use the word applies to the actions and counteractions of supernatural beings. "Legend" is its humanized counterpart: the recording of the deeds and doings of earthly heroes, whether or not they trod the ground with historic feet. "Lore" or "folklore" applies to everyday happenings: the joking on a powwow ground or at a church social; the contemporary stories that are told and retold so often that they lose any tribal identity.

In the history of the North American Indians there are more holes than fabric. That fabric must be pieced together from field, library, and archival research; from the unearthings of archaeologists and from ethnologists' interviews with living informants. In a sense the historian must be the final critic of the combining. It is his word, based on the records of other cultures, compared, evaluated, and enumerated, that the anthropologist-folklorist can and should accept. For if any tale be told from one side, and then from another, its truths must tally and its strands be firmly twisted.

In assembling this collection of myths, legends, and contemporary lore, the compilers have relied as much as possible on field data they themselves have collected, and only in rare instances have reproduced myths taken from other sources. In assembling the specimens to be photographed to illustrate the book, they have drawn on their own collections, on other collections in private hands, and on a few museum specimens.

Therefore the professional anthropologist, folklorist, or art historian should be cautioned—and hereby is—that many of the "classic" myths most often included in other collections have been omitted or presented in an unfamiliar form. The tired old "war horses" of North American Indian art, frequently used as illustrations in other volumes, are also absent. Both are available elsewhere. As much as possible, the compilers have attempted to assemble an original piece of work, and to give its parts the freshness with which they were heard or seen.

Anthropologists do not know all they wish to know about when, how, or from where in Asia American Indians first entered the New World. The anthropologists have the assurance of paleontologists that no type of prehuman remains have been found on the northern or the southern continent of the hemisphere. *Homo sapiens,* as far as present knowledge stands, is the only humanoid species that has occupied the Americas.

The fact that only remains of biologically modern man have so far been discovered in the New World indicates that the migrations which populated it took place in the last, or at least the latest, stage in the development of mankind. Men had become one biological species before the migrations began. Human subspecies could mate and intermate among themselves, at will and desire, when the New World was first populated.

The estimated dates for the arrival of the first of a long series of migrations into the Americas have varied from two thousand to ten thousand years before Christ. The latter date is more generally acceptable to anthropologists, and most of them agree that the migrations probably continued into the fourth century B.C.

The early travelers may have come a long way to reach the New World; some of them possibly from as far as central Asia. Some probably came the shorter distance from eastern Asia, and the possibility of raft transportation from the Pacific islands cannot yet be discarded.

The first groups of wanderers from Asia came with languages. They and their successors had knowledge of fire; they could make cordage from vegetable fibers or sinew, and weapons from stones. These earliest Americans had domesticated dogs but no other man-abiding animals. Certainly if they had language, they had mythologies.

Above all, these people crossed from one continent to the other with all the human feelings any of us know: fear and courage; love and its twin, hate; knowledge and dread of death, and delight at the conception and coming of new lives.

In the world left behind by the adventurers the wheel, the working and uses of metals, the sail, and writing had still to be invented, as did the domestication of most animals and of plants. None of these traits formed a part of the pioneers' intellectual baggage. And in the years and decades, centuries and millennia that followed their first arriving, throughout the lengthening sequence of later migrations, no American Indians have been known to have independently invented any of these things, except plant domestication and the working of soft metals into ornaments.

The migration pattern was not a simple west-to-east movement. Some groups followed the western mountain ranges from Alaska to Tierra del Fuego. Some stopped on the way; some turned back and reversed their steps to the northward along the coasts and rivers of the continents. In every place where the migrants settled there followed a period of learning to use and control their environments, and of adapting themselves to the ecology of the new area. In time, use and adaptation produced a series of widely varying cultures.

Probably a diversity of languages had existed before the groups left Asia. As one ethnic unit and then another spread and separated, came together and parted again, eight great linguistic stocks developed in North America. Among these eight stocks were divided the languages of more than two hundred ethnic units. Some languages were so closely related as to be mutually intelligible, true dialects of a mother tongue. In other instances, speakers of two different but related languages were unable to comprehend each other's words. And in still others, two languages of different stocks were used by neighboring groups until a sort of lingua franca was formed. The wide variety of speech among American Indian groups must never be forgotten, for it poses difficulties for the translators and transcribers of oral literature.

Materially and nonmaterially the descendants of the Asian migrants improved on many ancestral importations. Knowledge was expanded and elaborated from the original traits. Economic surpluses accumulated in some areas, notably those in which people practiced horticulture, to allow the luxuries of priesthoods, scholars, and artists, whom the rest of the people maintained.

It is probably by no accident of history that Angkor-Wat, the great city-states of Europe, and Canton, Foochong, and other Chinese cities rose to power in the same centuries—900–1100 A.D. The founding of the great American Indian theocratic dictatorships, with their huge cities and widespread influence over whole subcontinents, occurred in Mexico, in Middle America, and in Peru at the same time period that cities rose to power on other continents.

Somewhere in the air, it almost seems, was an impulse that led men all around the globe to build monuments to themselves in the form of cities of carved stone. It was only when the high civilizations of the New World had reached their florescence and had begun to decline of their own weight that recorded and recording Europeans first encountered and overthrew them.

Beyond the great centers of American Indian civilizations there stretched the hinterlands, what anthropologists like to call "areas of peripheral or marginal cultures." This technical nomenclature is based on the fact that as a culture trait spreads from its point of origin it changes, diminishes, and finally merges with another trait or traits. Its original identity and entity finally are lost. The trait eventually becomes so greatly altered that it can be identified with its point of origin only by intensive research. So with myths and legends, as well as with material culture traits.

In 1498 John and Sebastian Cabot, citizens of Venice who sailed under letters patent issued by Henry VII of England, landed on and explored the Newfoundland coast. Henry, believing that Columbus had reached Asia, commissioned the Cabots to find a northern water route to that continent, to bypass the southern Atlantic route presumably opened for Spain. The Cabots recorded the presence of "red men" on the coast and farther inland, but made no attempt at conquest or colonization. In the sense that the Cabots failed to find the hoped-for northwest passage, their voyage was a failure, but it did serve to give England some claim to North America.

Mexico fell to Hernando Cortes in 1521. The Inca empire of Peru surrendered to Francisco Pizarro in 1526. In each case the conquistadores dealt with centralized, unified governments, which had already subdued and consolidated minor ethnic groups. A firm base for Spanish operations in the northern subcontinent had been established at the Aztec capital of Tenochtitlan, now Mexico City.

In 1534 Jacques Cartier, again looking for a northwest passage to the Indies, landed at the mouth of the Saint Lawrence River. Cartier reported to Francis I of France that although he had failed to locate the longed-for shortcut, he had found a country that was rich and fertile, animals with fine pelts, and natives who were willing to trade. He recommended that a colony be established there, as it was, in 1536.

In 1539 De Soto invaded the Floridas, and in the following year Coronado entered the Southwest. These were both strictly military expeditions, of exploration and, if necessary, of conquest. Both faced enormous problems of distance and communication which, in the end, defeated De Soto. Coronado returned to report that the country to the north was poor in mineral wealth, but that it could be colonized by farmers. In 1598 Oñate established the first Spanish capital at the junction of the Chama and Rio Grande rivers, and set his colonists to work on the land.

Whatever their nationalities, the first Europeans had a common language in Latin. They had writing in that tongue and in their own several languages, and the urge to write. Even when they wrote of their own activities, they could not omit mention of the natives of the country.

In different ways, the Indian cultures the Spaniards encountered in both the Southeast and the Southwest were marginal to the great Mayan and Aztec cultures of Mexico. They probably embody the return migrations from south to north which have already been mentioned. This is particularly clear-cut in the Southeast. Art forms, clothing and ornaments, an emphasis on the value of pearls and other semiprecious stones, with some knowledge of the working of copper into ornaments, characterized the Indians of the farm towns De Soto observed from the Gulf of Mexico to the Mississippi.

In New Mexico and Arizona the Indians cultivated maize of different types from those grown in Mexico and the Southeast. These Indians used much native turquoise, and sent expeditions to the Gulf of California to bring back shells to be worked into ornaments. Houses were built of puddled adobe or of stone. In both areas houses and town plans closely resembled those of the Aztec cities.

Probably the horticultural population of the Southwest had entered their area at an earlier period than their fellow farmers in the Southeast. Data on both migrations are still accumulating, and there still is no positive answer as to which southern-influenced culture was first developed.

As they were marginal materially, the first explored areas were also marginal to the religion, legends, and folklore of central Mexico. Temples in the Southeast were built on earth mounds instead of on stone pyramids, and houses were of locally available wattle-and-daub construction materials instead of stone, for instance. In the Southwest, temples had disappeared, to be replaced by kivas, underground places of worship.

In both areas a pantheon so elaborate that only professional theologians could understand or explain it had been simplified into an over-all abiding power of good, matched by an equally strong power of evil. Both supernatural beings worked through a multitude of nature spirits, some of them guardians of man, some of them inimical to him. A system of astronomy based on solar and lunar observations and highly developed mathematics had slipped into simple observations of the solstices and the equinoxes.

Firmly binding together the earliest Europeans to settle the New World was a single faith. Spaniards and Frenchmen were alike Roman Catholics. The Reformation had begun in Europe, but these men were of the Roman Catholic Church. The auto-da-fé and the Inquisition were part of the daily life of Spain. Some French explorer-soldier-colonists had fought against the Protestants in the Netherlands and the Huguenots at home.

The chaplains traveled with the armies or settled with the colonists, and they, too, wrote their accounts of conquest, of the overcoming of devils and putting to death of stubborn heathen who adhered to their old pagan beliefs in the face of the preaching of the word of the God of peace.

The French priests were less totalitarian and more realistic in their dealings with the Indians than were the Spanish. The priests who accompanied Cartier, La Salle, and Joliet were men of considerable physical strength and endurance, who had been especially trained to reinforce their strengthening faith by physically facing frontier hardships before they left France.

These French priests preached, in general, a loving God. They baptized the Indians without arguing with them, and, so long as "pagan rites" were not held in public and so forced on their attention, the Frenchmen usually did not create crises.

Throughout French Canada, around the Great Lakes, and down the Mississippi, wherever French soldiers and *voyageurs* took their canoes, for the French were water-borne as were the Indians they met, the explorers met and married Indian women. There were large families of mixed blood in New France before the beginning of the eighteenth century, many of them comprised of men and women of high intelligence and ability. It was not necessary to destroy in order to overcome, in the French colonization philosophy. The whole process could be accomplished efficiently by letting nature take its course. And the part-French children were naturally raised in the Catholic Church, and just as naturally paid little or no attention to the "fairy stories" told them by their Indian mothers and grandmothers.

But in the Southwest the military chaplains ruled with an iron hand. Whole villages were baptized en masse, lest the population should continue as *gentes sin raison*—people without minds or souls. The Spanish policy demanded that they be given souls in the Spanish sense, whether the Indians wanted souls or not. At the same time, the Indians were given Spanish names which were to supersede their Tewa, Piro, Keres, or Hopi ones. A new God had been introduced, and his precepts were to be mercilessly followed, even to the extent of blotting out the native names of towns with the names of saints.

At Acoma Pueblo, situated on the top of a five-hundred-foot mesa and drawing its water supply from natural rock cisterns, Indian women climbed paths that were no more than toe holds, carrying baskets of earth and jars of water on their heads, until the Church of St. Stephen, one of the largest adobe structures in the Southwest, stood proudly against the sky. A filled-in earth graveyard with an adobe wall, adorned with effigies of helmeted heads, fronted the church on the flat rock of the mesa top. How many of those laboring women, one wonders, were among the first to lay their weary bones in the earth the padres had commanded them to carry?

Formerly the Pueblos had been theocratic. The cacique and his assistants controlled the lives of the people. The effect of Spanish conquest was not to destroy the native government and religion, as the French had done by attrition, but to drive them underground. The religion and government of the village Indians certainly did not disappear from the earth.

In 1958 the governor of a Rio Grande pueblo was explaining one of his paintings to the Roman Catholic archbishop who had honored the village with a pontifical High Mass.

"What does the symbol in the corner represent?" the churchman inquired.

"Your Excellency, that is the Moon God we worship," was the bland reply.

Not all of the southwestern village Indians were so adaptable as the Tewas and Keres had been in the beginning. At Awatobi and Oraibi the Hopis simply dropped the Spanish priests over the mesa cliffs. At Zuni the priests were crucified head down, and the church was destroyed. These priests certainly were as brave and hardy as the French, and they suffered for their faith.

In 1680 all the Rio Grande Pueblos, under the leadership of Popé, a native of San Juan who had located his base of operations at Taos, rose in concerted rebellion and drove the Spaniards back into Mexico. In 1692, under Francisco de Vargas, the Spaniards reconquered New Mexico. The Indians were subdued there once and for all.

Myths and legends, in the Indian phrase, went underground, into the kivas. The great myths were still known and taught, but only the "little stories," the how and why tales, were told out loud. To all appearances the eastern villages of the Southwest had become and remained Catholic.

The marauding Navahos and Apaches, Athabascan-speaking tribes who had come out of the Northwest into the Southwest in the thirteenth century, were less affected by the Spanish invasion, at first, than were the villagers. These peoples were drifting and remote; there was apparently nothing in the desert and mountain country they occupied that anybody else could possibly want at that time. So the Athabascans continued to hold their night- and day-long healing ceremonials, each of which required the recital of myths and the singing of hymns, without interruption. Athabascan culture was influenced by Spanish horses, burros, and sheep, but not by religion. This explains why so much more of Athabascan than of other Indian religion, ritual, and mythology has survived to this day.

Englishmen finally settled on the Virginia coast in 1607. They were landless younger sons in the main, ambitiously searching for the property denied them in their homeland, and they were of the Church of England. The English were far less set on missionary work among the southeastern tribes than were the Spaniards or the French in their areas.

The English policy toward the southeastern Indians was simply to move them aside and occupy their property. If the "red men" objected to moving, that was unfortunate, but the misfortune could be overcome with guns and gunpowder. A simple policy of elimination predominated; when the Indians would not eliminate themselves by transfer, the English obligingly did it for them with superior weapons.

The English colonists of the next wave, in the Northeast, did not even attempt elimination by moving. The Pilgrim fathers were glad of the assistance and food given them by the Narragansets when the first colonists landed in Massachusetts. Their relations with the Indians remained tolerant for several years, although William Bradford foreshadowed the future when he found himself "sorely put to know what these heathen people did in Truth believe, that they should cling to it."

Later the Puritans, bent on purifying the already rigid Protestantism of the Pilgrim fathers, set in action a "convert or fight" program of their own. Cotton Mather was not a man who hesitated to press those accused of witchcraft to death between stone slabs, or to hang convicted witches on village commons. He and his adherents could not be expected to treat the Indians with any greater kindness and tolerance than they did those members of their own society who displeased them.

Even in Quaker Pennsylvania, the gentler Friends gave up the effort to "convert the heathen" through their own love of humanity and sweet reasonableness. Here the Englishmen made treaties with the Indians, and then occupied their land. The Indians could move away or farm like Englishmen. Most of the Delawares chose the former course.

The effect of settlement on Indian religions was the same everywhere in the English colonies. The Englishmen admired the practicality of the log structure of Iroquois long houses. That there might be a religious purpose behind the long-house construction, or that the building might mean more than physical shelter to its occupants, escaped the English. All of Iroquoian social and religious life centered in the long house, but the building was dwelling place as well as place of worship.

As with the flint-and-steel firelighters, the guns and gunpowder, and the metal axes the English had brought with them, all of which the Indians readily adopted, the materially superior trait was accepted by the invaders. Log houses and cabins became the favorite habitations of English-descended frontiersmen.

New religions arose among the eastern tribes, particularly among the Algonkians and Iroquois, blending with and succeeding one another, and impartially incorporating elements of Christianity. To the south of the Ohio River the Caddoan Pawnees and the Siouan Osages and Omahas were fortunate in preserving their world views and beliefs almost intact into the twentieth century. These groups were on the remote western frontier of the French and English lands, the equally remote eastern frontier of the Spanish possessions.

The middle Mississippi tribes, in early years, had far less direct contact with Europeans than the groups surrounding them. They could preserve their sacred myths longer than Indians in other areas.

There was another trait besides writing and Christianity that all Europeans—Spanish, French, English or other—had in common. They all believed in land as *property to be owned.* A man's worth and wealth could be counted with the acres he controlled. The land was a European's individual property. He owned it. He could buy it and sell it. He could give or bequeath it to his children, and they in turn to theirs.

This European landownership concept was so strange to all the Indians that it was literally incomprehensible. The land was *there,* they said, and that was what mattered. Each tribe or village knew the boundaries of its corn fields and hunting territories. But the Indians knew the boundaries as defining the space they themselves used from that which their neighbors needed. Boundaries between Indian nations were not fences around jealously-held private lands.

Ruth Benedict expressed the matter most clearly in her *Counters in the Game:* ''Land? What use was more land than would feed him to any man? If these white-faced strangers wanted land and nothing else, let it be given to them.''

The point of separation of the two land concepts was precisely that the Europeans *did* want more land than would feed them. Behind them, as they sailed westward or struggled northward, they had left a continent already so overcrowded that it could not feed its exploding populations. Land, and more land, they wanted.

When the colonists of the eastern seaboard rose against the English government, the new United States filled with white men's towns and swarmed with the people who were descended from the earlier Europeans or were newcomers from over the seas. The space between the Atlantic seaboard and the Mississippi River was rapidly filling. The new United States adopted a ruthless Indian policy: removal, enclosure, or extermination of the no-good red devils.

Westward pressure from the emigrants pushed Indian groups always farther inland and always closer together. Quarrels over occupied and invaded hunting lands grew into tribal wars. The white men encouraged the divisions between Indian groups and within the group structures.

Additionally, each European ethnic group had its quarrels with others, and had brought these disagreements to the New World with them. Wars in North America had inevitably repeated Old World struggles. Whites enlisted allies on either side by deliberately pitting tribe against tribe. Division and conquest were accomplished simultaneously.

The coastal Algonkians moved inland from the Atlantic, up the westward flowing rivers, for they were accustomed to using canoes, and water routes were their preferred ways.

Ultimately, the Delawares and Micmacs reached the Great Lakes. Some bands remained there and made common cause with the Algonkian-speaking Ojibway, Pottawatomie, Sauk, Fox, and Kickapoo, and with the Siouan-speaking Santee and Winnebago. While other bands moved on, the Great Lakes Algonkians and Siouans merged their cultures in a blend that anthropologists today have a hard time separating into its original components. As happened elsewhere, a lingua franca between disparate linguistic stocks was formed.

On the Gulf coast, the Muskoghean-speaking Choctaws acquired horses from the English settlers before 1702. The French explorer Bienville in that year spoke of the hoof beats of Choctaw ponies, trotting along the riverside trails which these natural and international traders followed to the north and west, taking with them Mobilian, which language tribes unrelated to Muskoghean speakers could comprehend.

Stallions and mules had come into the southwest with Coronado and his army. Oñate's later colonists brought brood mares, and bred horses as they did cattle and sheep. Indians acquired the offspring of Spanish horse-breeding by stealth rather than by trade. Descendants of the Spanish herds, straying from their original or acquisitive owners onto the open grasslands at the heart of the continent, actually created the Plains Indian culture of the eighteenth and nineteenth centuries.

Once the inland Indians had horses there occurred an explosion from the horticultural-hunting villages of the Mississippi drainage, as far west as the headwaters of the Arkansas and Canadian rivers. Mounted Indians invaded the inland ocean of the plains, across which herds of buffalo drifted and grazed like schools of whales.

Once the buffalo had had to be hunted singly and by stealth, or driven in masses over cliffs, to dash themselves to a struggling pulp on the rocks below. Now, Indian hunters on horseback could ride into the buffalo herds, select the best animals, and kill them with arrows or lances. For a time, as the Cheyenne and Arapaho, the Brule, Miniconju, Hunkpapa, Oglala and other Dakotas, the Kiowas and Comanches, and the Osages, Otos, Poncas, and Pawnees took to the plains, the pressure against the northern and central tribes was eased and those groups could shift westward.

White pressure was soon felt again, as it covered a mappable hundred miles each ten years. Tribe was pushed against tribe, with resulting outbreaks of hostility between them. Some Indian groups were exterminated; some merged for protection with other, stronger tribes. And still other Indian tribes, downfacing all enemies, have maintained their identities to the present day.

Whatever the survival capacity and tenacity of the Indians themselves during the period of expansion, no one but the Indians paid any attention to Indian religion, art, music, drama, or poetry except to decry it as pagan and primitive. White men created a Bureau of Indian Affairs, to "protect" the Indians. At the same time, white men continued to urge the Indians to throw the old ways aside, and to replace them with the faiths and skills of the Euro-Americans. The nonmaterial culture traits of the invaders, because they *were* of European origin, must be as superior to those of the aboriginies as the wheel-based Euro-American culture was mechanically to the pole-and-lever engineering of the Indians.

Time passed, hurrying through the shortening centuries. Much Indian knowledge and literature was lost and gone forever. Then, suddenly, there was a stirring among the intellectuals in the cities and universities of the eastern United States. Curiosity about the Indians was aroused.

For the first time, in the 1830s, scholars realized that these Indians were *people*. They were human beings. Surely the Indians must have belief and knowledge, as other peoples had. The too-well-named brothers Grimm in Germany, Hauff in Austria, and Perrault in France were recording the lore and customs of the peasants of their own countries. Hans Christian Andersen was assembling for the world the folk tales of the Danes. Perhaps there were New World parallels for these collections.

Such men as the Philadelphia miniaturist George Catlin, the administrator Henry Rowe Schoolcraft, the lawyer Lewis Henry Morgan, and the journalist Washington Irving traveled west. Sprigs of English and Continental aristocracy included the western United States in their *grands tours,* bringing their staff artists with them. These men set down their observations of the Indians' customs and habits in words and pictures. Their records are invaluable to present-day scholars.

A new science, anthropology, conceived out of geology by philosophy, embraced the physical and nonphysical aspects of man. The subject was taught in European universities. Anthropology's westward spread was as inevitable to the knowledge-hungry of the New World as the spread of settlement had been to men hungry for new lands.

What we know now of Indian religions, of the myths they inspired and of the legends the Indians created around their semihistorical heroes, is fragmentary at best. The material was first recorded by men of intellectual curiosity because it *was* curious. Much that seemed to them everyday and ordinary, the repetitious round of daily life of women, for instance, slipped by them unrecorded.

Later workers, Franz Boas, John Swanton, Truman Michelson, and Frank Speck among them, studied the languages in which the Indians' stories were told. These men recorded volume after notebook of tribal myths and legends, sometimes supplying literal textual translations of their informants' words.

Stith Thompson, in the early twentieth century, brought myths from many tribes together for study and comparison. Alfred Kroeber noted similarities between certain Asiatic and American Indian myth themes. Stephen Barrett commented on the resemblance of Machabo, the Great Hare of the Algonkian myths, to the Br'er Rabbit tales brought to the southern states by African Negro slaves.

All these scholars alike wrote primarily for their brother scholars. They were fast on the trail of vanishing knowledge. Record! Record! Record! was their cry. Time enough for detailed analysis, synthesis, and discussion of aesthetic qualities later.

As a result, while the field work of the early American professional anthropologists was superbly scholarly, it was often unreadable except by other anthropologists, or by a few folklorists who laboriously wound their way through the phonetic jungles, to arrive at last at the gist of some half-forgotten tale, told in bits and pieces by men and women grown too old to remember the myth's ramifications, entirety, or context. Much of what was recorded early in this century still remains in musty field notebooks, untranscribed.

It must be stated, too, that the field anthropologist is always at the mercy of his interpreters. Many informants whose English is adequate for story telling still insist on having their spokesmen. If this be a person familiar with the best of his own language and of English, or one who is fascinated by the *idea* of languages and their words, well and good. A satisfactory translation will result. But if he be someone who is indifferent to nuances of meanings; to whom words, as to Molière's character, are prose spoken all his life, then it is up to the field worker to fill in with comparative data, or to draw on his own knowledge of the mores of a given group.

Yet the great genius shared by all American Indians was and remains verbal and oral. Since the Indians lacked writing to record their philosophies and literatures, they played with the spoken word, combining and recombining phrases and thoughts.

North American Indians, wherever they lived, delivered orations, made the poems and music of songs, and created four-day-long miracle plays. Their two-hour-long ritual prayers had to be recited without an error or the omission of a single syllable, else the spell would not be cast, the ceremony would fail, and life-giving rain and snow, crops, or wild game herds would not come to the aid of men that season.

To sit in a tribal council meeting, even today, is to hear oratory, although it is as often delivered in English as in the speaker's ancestral language.

To endure through a long winter's night the solemn recitation of prayers and invocations to the gods at a Zuñi Shalako ceremony is to be impressed forever by the grace of men's speech, even though that speech be incomprehensible as words.

To watch and listen in a white canvas tipi while priests and people night long sing to Jesus and partake of the peyote sacrament is to know an enduring depth of religious feeling.

And to sit in the full blaze of an August sun on baking rocks, while Hopi priests move through the meeting and countermeeting of two groups of musicians in a Flute Ceremony, is to realize painfully our loss when this music cannot be and that of other groups has not been recorded.

From reconstructed fragments of auditory archaeology, then, the myths and legends that appear in this book have been compiled. Many of them appear as the original field work of the compilers. They were recorded in hospital wards, beside country kitchen wood stoves, in the swamps while gathering rushes to be plaited into mats, in our own living rooms, and at powwows.

In some cases the compilers have drawn on the published works of other anthropologists and when necessary have reworded literally-translated myths and legends into something that seems to them a nearer expression of the grace and beauty of the Indians' spoken words. The intention throughout the book is to present stories for what they are: a body of unwritten literature, but literature nonetheless.

Some concrete statements have emerged from the gleanings. The Indian world is divided by fours: four seasons, four divisions of a day or a life, and, above all, four World Corners—the cardinal or semicardinal directions. Certain type-characters are almost universally distributed among the American Indians north of Mexico. Among them are the Hero, the Trickster, the Trickster-Hero who brings together traits of each of the others, the Grandmother Spider, and her grandsons, the Twin War Gods.

The Culture Hero stands for the strength, wisdom, and perception of men. He is not the Power Above, but he is the intermediary between that Power and mankind. He protects women and children from harm; he sends power visions to youths; he steps between men and nature when no one else can.

The Trickster per se is used to explain natural phenomena, especially those from which a moral can be drawn. He makes trouble. He displays disagreeable traits, like greediness. He is often the central character in stories that are best termed ethno-pornography, and which are so gratuitously repetitious and detailed that they have been omitted from this volume. The Trickster is Eros plus Pan.

The Trickster-Hero has no precise European analogy. He is a cross between Til Eulenspiegl and Prometheus. Known under many names in many tribes, he sometimes does good intentionally, sometimes by accident. In his Trickster manifestation the Trickster-Hero deliberately wreaks mischief, havoc, and in extreme cases, chaos. In his heroic manifestation he defeats death, or brings food to the people.

Grandmother Spider is all of womankind, Eve and Lilith in one, old to begin with wherever we meet her although she is capable of transforming herself into a young and beautiful woman when she wishes. Spider Woman lives alone, or with her grandsons between their adventures. Grandmother Spider directs men's thoughts and destinies through her kindness and wise advice, or lures to the underworld those whose thoughts and actions seem to her profane.

The War Twins are harder to define than the other type-characters. Through them we perceive the duality basic to all men and all religions. The Twins are young, but they can suddenly become old. One is good and one is bad. The Hopis say that the Twins face each other from the north and south—''poles'' is added today—and their balance keeps the world steady on its axis. The Twins are killers of enemies, and sometimes of enemy gods. They are the personification of action, not of contemplation. Always they are of supernatural parentage on at least one side, and often they are virgin-born.

Predominantly the War Twins are human. Their very humanity is their appeal and their puzzle. The War Twins brought safety and harmony into the world through their destruction of enemy gods, and are often described as homosexual, with as many female as male traits. Twin babies—or at least one of a pair of twins—in the past seldom survived the first twenty-four hours of life in certain Indian tribes. The duality of adult personalities must not be permitted to develop.

Beyond the type-characters and at the core of all North American Indian religions there is a complex spirit concept. Above and beyond all the powers of nature there is a Creator, a divine being who makes men out of the dust of the earth or the mud of lake or river bottoms. He is the One, the All-in-All, the Being who has been denominated by white men as the Great Spirit.

Under the Creator's direction and within His guidance are a host of other supernatural beings, all great, none supreme. Sun is father and Earth mother of us all. Exposure to the sun and contact with the earth bring strength and blessing. Winds, rain, clouds, thunder, and storms are Sun and Earth's means of communication with each other and with mankind. The importance of moon and stars seems to vary from tribe to tribe, although the variation may be due to the lacunae of time. Solstices, equinoxes, and eclipses never cease to arouse awe and wonder, and are to be regarded as the work of the many spirits.

Rivers and mountains, deserts and fields, stones and running water, animals and plants and human beings all are endowed with protective power in North American Indian beliefs. Sometimes the aid of the good spirits can be obtained through fasting, suffering, and prayer. Sometimes the blessing comes without a man's seeking it, as a revelation of his own innate power as an individual.

Power, the animating force of the universe, derives from the Creator and His helpers. There is no other English word which even partially conveys what most Indians mean when they say ''Power.'' Perhaps ''talent'' or ''genius,'' when the word is applied to an individual, most nearly approaches the meaning Indians give to the word Power.

In the world views of most North American Indians there are worlds beyond this one. Sometimes, as in the Pawnee cosmology, there are worlds outside the one that men live in, enclosing the human world within like the shell of a river mussel or the curve of an earth lodge. Sometimes we can discern a clearly stated concept of an after life, as in the Hopi belief in a valley below a lake where the good eternally rejoice, and which the wicked eternally strive to reach by crossing a thorn-strewn desert. In other mythologies the after-life concept seems to have been lost, if, indeed, it ever existed. The Kiowas are a case in point; the great appeal of Christianity to them was the rewarding of goodness; previously the Kiowas believed that only the wicked survived, in the form of owls.

Research and analysis of materials have convinced the compilers that myths and legends repeat from culture area to culture area and from tribe to tribe, varying principally with regional ecologies. Machabo, the Trickster-Hero of the Algonkians, is a woodland creature; Old Man Coyote of the Comanches is a Trickster-Hero of the western plains and mountains, for instance. If the stories that follow seem heavily weighted in the direction of certain tribes, it is because those are the tribes with whom the compilers have worked first hand, not because the same stories do not appear elsewhere.

Only by being read in the contexts of the societies in which they developed can the values of any myths be distinguished, whenever or wherever the myths occur. For this reason brief descriptions of the cultures have been included, with mention of tribal names, linguistic stocks, and the culture traits that at once link and separate geographical areas from each other.

Out of this collection of material the compilers hope that there will emerge a clearer understanding of the patterns of North American Indian religions and their mythologies, and of the philosophies which myths and legends embody. It will be incomplete. But let the stories be told as stories, beautiful in themselves, and in their relationships to the lives of the original tellers.

Part One
THE WORLD BEYOND OURS

How the World Was Made

The Algonkian-speaking Cheyenne came out of the woodlands west of the Great Lakes, and on to the central plains in the mid-seventeenth century. The Cheyennes quickly abandoned agriculture and the crafts that require sedentary life in favor of buffalo hunting and horseback life.

By the beginning of the eighteenth century the Cheyennes had become known as the prototype of the horseback Indians of the plains: bold, dashing, feather-crowned warriors who raided other tribes and brought home women and wealth. When the opportunity offered, Cheyenne raiders also attacked white settlements and forts.

Life on the plains was made possible for the Cheyennes by the existence of a single animal: the buffalo. Its flesh furnished food, its hide furnished tipi covers, clothing, shoes, and containers, and any part of its body could be used ceremonially. The summer Sun Dance, greatest of all Cheyenne ceremonies, was intended to keep the buffalo alive so that all the people might live.

Cheyenne women were skilled craftsworkers—first with paints and porcupine quills, later, after white trade become established, with beads.

However much their physical life changed, the Cheyenne retained their old mythological pattern, and never lost the basic concepts they had brought to the plains with them. The story that follows is typical of origin myths in general whether of the tribes of the woodlands or of those who reached the plains.

▼▼▼▼▼

In the beginning there was nothing, and Maheo, the All Spirit, lived in the void. He looked around him, but there was nothing to see. He listened, but there was nothing to hear. There was only Maheo, alone in nothingness.

Because of the greatness of his Power, Maheo was not lonesome. His being was a Universe. But as he moved through the endless time of nothingness, it seemed to Maheo that his Power should be put to use. What good is Power, Maheo asked himself, if it is not used to make a world and people to live in it?

With his Power, Maheo created a great water, like a lake, but salty. Out of this salty water, Maheo knew, he could bring all life that ever was to be. The lake itself was life, if Maheo so commanded it. In the darkness of nothingness, Maheo could feel the coolness of the water and taste on his lips the tang of the salt.

"There should be water beings," Maheo told his Power. And so it was. First the fish, swimming in the deep water, and then the mussels and snails and crawfish, lying on the sand and mud Maheo had formed so his lake should have a bottom.

Let us also create something that lives on the water, Maheo thought to his Power.

And so it was. For now there were snow geese, and mallards and teal and coots and terns and loons living and swimming about on the water's surface. Maheo could hear the splashing of their feet and the flapping of their wings in the darkness.

I should like to see the things that have been created, Maheo decided.

And, again, so it was. Light began to grow and spread, first white and bleached in the east, then golden and strong till it filled the middle of the sky and extended all around the horizon. Maheo watched the light, and he saw the birds and fishes, and the shellfish lying on the bottom of the lake as the light showed them to him.

How beautiful it all is, Maheo thought in his heart.

Then the snow goose paddled over to where she thought Maheo was, in the space above the lake. "I do not see You, but I know that

You exist,'' the goose began. "I do not know where You are, but I know You must be everywhere. Listen to me, Maheo. This is good water that You have made, on which we live. But birds are not like fish. Sometimes we get tired swimming. Sometimes we would like to get out of the water.''

"Then fly,'' said Maheo, and he waved his arms, and all the water birds flew, skittering along the surface of the lake until they had speed enough to rise in the air. The skies were darkened with them.

"How beautiful their wings are in the light,'' Maheo said to his Power, as the birds wheeled and turned, and became living patterns against the sky.

The loon was the first to drop back to the surface of the lake. "Maheo,'' he said, looking around, for he knew that Maheo was all about him, "You have made us sky and light to fly in, and You have made us water to swim in. It sounds ungrateful to want something else, yet still we do. When we are tired of swimming and tired of flying, we should like a dry solid place where we could walk and rest. Give us a place to build our nests, please, Maheo.''

"So be it,'' answered Maheo, "but to make such a place I must have your help, all of you. By myself, I have made four things: the water, the light, the sky air, and the peoples of the water. Now I must have help if I am to create more, for my Power will only let me make four things by myself.''

"Tell us how we can help You,'' said all the water peoples. "We are ready to do what You say.''

Maheo stretched out his hand and beckoned. "Let the biggest and the swiftest try to find land first,'' he said, and the snow goose came to him.

"I am ready to try,'' the snow goose said, and she drove herself along the water until the white wake behind her grew and grew to a sharp white point that drove her up into the air as the feathers drive an arrow. She flew high into the sky, until she was only a dark spot against the clearness of the light. Then the goose turned, and down she plunged, faster than any arrow, and dived into the water. She pierced the surface with her beak as if it were the point of a spear.

The snow goose was gone a long time. Maheo counted to four four hundred times before she rose to the surface of the water and lay there floating, her beak half open as she gasped for air.

"What have you brought us?'' Maheo asked her, and the snow goose sighed sadly, and answered, "Nothing. I brought nothing back.''

Then the loon tried, and after him, the mallard. Each in turn rose until he was a speck against the light, and turned and dived with the speed of a flashing arrow into the water. And each in turn rose wearily, and wearily answered, "Nothing," when Maheo asked him what he had brought.

At last there came the little coot, paddling across the surface of the water very quietly, dipping his head sometimes to catch a tiny fish, and shaking the water beads from his scalp lock whenever he rose.

"Maheo," the little coot said softly, "when I put my head beneath the water, it seems to me that I see something there, far below. Perhaps I can swim down to it—I don't know. I can't fly or dive like my sister and brothers. All I can do is swim, but I will swim down the best I know how, and go as deep as I can. May I try, please, Maheo?"

"Little brother," said Maheo, "no man can do more than his best, and I have asked for the help of all the water peoples. Certainly you shall try. Perhaps swimming will be better than diving, after all. Try, little brother, and see what you can do."

"Hah-ho!" the little coot said. "Thank you, Maheo," and he put his head under the water and swam down and down and down and down, until he was out of sight.

The coot was gone a long, long, long, long time. Then Maheo and the other birds could see a little dark spot beneath the water's surface, slowly rising toward them. It seemed as if they would never see the coot himself, but at last the spot began to have a shape. Still it rose and rose, and at last Maheo and the water peoples could surely see who it was. The little coot was swimming up from the bottom of the salty lake.

When the coot reached the surface, he stretched his closed beak upward into the light, but he did not open it.

"Give me what you have brought," Maheo said, and the coot let his beak fall open, so a little ball of mud could fall from his tongue into Maheo's hand, for when Maheo wanted to, he could become like a man.

"Go, little brother," Maheo said. "Thank you, and may what you have brought always protect you."

And so it was and so it is, for the coot's flesh still tastes of mud, and neither man nor animal will eat a coot unless there is nothing else to eat.

Maheo rolled the ball of mud between the palms of his hands, and it began to grow larger, until there was almost too much mud for Maheo to hold. He looked around for a place to put the mud, but there was nothing but water or air anywhere around him.

"Come and help me again, water peoples," Maheo called. "I must put this mud somewhere. One of you must let me place it on his back.''

All the fish and all the other water creatures came swimming to Maheo, and he tried to find the right one to carry the mud. The mussels and snails and crawfish were too small, although they all had solid backs, and they lived too deep in the water for the mud to rest on them. The fish were too narrow, and their back fins stuck up through the mud and cut it to pieces. Finally only one water person was left.

''Grandmother Turtle,'' Maheo asked, ''do you think that you can help me?''

''I'm very old and very slow, but I will try,'' the turtle answered. She swam over to Maheo, and he piled the mud on her rounded back, until he had made a hill. Under Maheo's hands the hill grew and spread and flattened out, until the Grandmother Turtle was hidden from sight.

''So be it,'' Maheo said once again. ''Let the earth be known as our Grandmother, and let the Grandmother who carries the earth be the only being who is at home beneath the water, or within the earth, or above the ground; the only one who can go anywhere by swimming or by walking as she chooses.''

And so it was, and so it is. Grandmother Turtle and all her descendants must walk very slowly, for they carry the whole weight of the whole world and all its peoples on their backs.

Now there was earth as well as water, but the earth was barren. And Maheo said to his Power, ''Our Grandmother Earth is like a woman; she should be fruitful. Let her begin to bear life. Help me, my Power.''

When Maheo said that, trees and grass sprang up to become the Grandmother's hair. The flowers became her bright ornaments, and the fruits and the seeds were the gifts that the earth offered back to Maheo. The birds came to rest on her hands when they were tired, and the fish came close to her sides. Maheo looked at the Earth Woman and he thought she was very beautiful; the most beautiful thing he had made so far.

She should not be alone, Maheo thought. Let me give her something of myself, so she will know that I am near her and that I love her.

Maheo reached into his right side, and pulled out a rib bone. He breathed on the bone, and laid it softly on the bosom of the Earth Woman. The bone moved and stirred, stood upright and walked. The first man had come to be.

''He is alone with the Grandmother Earth as I once was alone with the void," said Maheo. "It is not good for anyone to be alone." So Maheo fashioned a human woman from his left rib, and set her with the man. Then there were two persons on the Grandmother Earth, her children and Maheo's. They were happy together, and Maheo was happy as he watched them.

After a year, in the springtime, the first child was born. As the years passed, there were other children. They went their ways, and founded many tribes.

From time to time, after that, Maheo realized that his people walking on the earth had certain needs. At those times, Maheo, with the help of his Power, created animals to feed and care for the people. He gave them deer for clothing and food, porcupines to make their ornaments, the swift antelopes on the open plains, and the prairie dogs that burrowed in the earth.

At last Maheo thought to his Power, Why, one animal can take the place of all the others put together, and then he made the buffalo.

Maheo is still with us. He is everywhere, watching all his people, and all the creation he has made. Maheo is all good and all life; he is the creator, the guardian, and the teacher. We are all here because of Maheo.

▼▼▼▼▼

As told to Alice Marriott and Carol K. Rachlin by Mary Little Bear Inkanish, Cheyenne, 1960.

How the World Was Made

The Modocs today live in their native area, at the foot of the eastern slope of the Cascade Mountains, in Oregon, in the series of broken, jagged volcanic valleys leading out to the great desert plateau of extreme eastern Oregon and western Nevada. It is a country cut through with rivers running into lakes.

Modoc life depended on valleys, rivers, and lakes in that order. The Modocs dug camas lily and wild turnip roots with pointed sticks, and each band knew its assigned digging area and valley floor. There the Modocs gathered the seeds of wild plants and hunted large and small game. From the rivers came salmon and other fish, which were smoke-dried and stored for winter use. From the rivers also came turtles, whose flesh was eaten and whose shells were used for bowls and utensils. The lakes furnished wild water lily roots in spring, and lily seeds in fall. Tules, or rushes, grew along the lake shores, and were woven into mats, baskets, moccasins, or used as thatch to roof the semi-subterranean houses where the Modocs lived in winter.

The Modoc concept of the world and of its coming to be was a simple one. It did not try to explain all natural phenomena, with the philosophical detail of the Cheyenne story of the creation. Nor were the Modocs skeptical of supernatural power like those most penetrating

27

agnostics, the Comanches. The world was and is, and the Modoc Cul-
ture Hero made it. You can still see the rock on the east shore of dry
Tule Lake in the northern California, and the hole through it which
Kumokums made so he could look out at the rest of the world.

▼▼▼▼▼

Kumokums was the one that made the world and everything that is in
it. This is how he did it.

Kumokums sat down beside Tule Lake, on its east shore. He was
not afraid, but he was interested, because there was nothing anywhere
but Tule Lake.

That's a lot of water, Kumokums said to himself. I wonder how
it would look if it had some land around it?

So he reached down, down, down, down, down, five times, to the
bottom of Tule Lake, and the fifth time he reached, Kumokums drew
up a handful of mud. He piled it up in front of him, like a hill, and
patted it with the palm of his hand.

As Kumokums patted the mud, it began to spread beneath his
hand, out and around him, until Tule Lake was completely surrounded by earth, and Kumokums was left sitting on a little island of
mud in the middle of the water.

"Well!" said Kumokums. "I didn't know it would do that."

So he drew back some of the earth on the west and the north, to
make the mountains. He cut grooves in the mountain sides with his
fingernail, so the rivers could flow down to the lakes. That is why you
should bury your fingernail parings, or throw them back into the
water, so they will return to Kumokums.

Kumokums drew trees and plants out of the earth, and he put
birds in the air, fish in the water, and animals on the land. He had
shaped and decorated the world as a woman shapes and decorates a
basket.

Then Kumokums was tired. He had done everything he could
think of to do, and winter was about to begin.

I will do what the bear does, Kumokums thought. I will make
myself a hole where I will be safe, and sleep the winter through.

Kumokums dug himself a hole under the bottom of Tule Lake,
with the hill where he had created the world to mark the spot. By now
the hill had dried out and turned to solid rock, as it is today.

Just at the last moment, as he was about to go underground,
Kumokums thought, I might want to look out sometime and see what
is going on, without bothering to move around. So he scratched and

scratched with his fingernail until he had made a hole in the rock, near its top, that was big enough to see through. It is still there, and people can climb the rock and look out through the hole, all around the country, for Tule Lake dried up and became planted land many years ago.

But some day Kumokums will surely wake up, and when he looks out and sees how his world has changed, perhaps he will bring the water back to the floor of Tule Lake, and things will again be as they were when Kumokums first made them.

▼▼▼▼▼▼

As told to Alice Marriott by Evangeline Schonchin, translated by Mary Chiloquin, Modocs.

Also included in: Ray, Verne F., Primitive Pragmatists, The Modoc Indians of Northern California. *Seattle: University of Washington Press, 1963.*

How the Sun Came

The southeastern quadrant of the United States was the first area permanently occupied by non-Indians to the exclusion of the Indians.

The English colonists did not pursue a stated formal policy of extermination toward the Indians, but the effect of their land use was as devastating as if they had. The southern Indians were pushed westward, first into the highlands of Tennessee and the Carolinas. Later, the Indians were removed across the Mississippi and the Indian Territory was established in what is now eastern Oklahoma.

That any fragments of culture should have survived this four-century process of extermination and removal is astonishing. It is also indicative of much that is Indian in character: determination, clinging to tradition, and respect for the elders and the old ways. The myth that follows is a Cherokee version of the sun-catching myth found everywhere in the United States, and one of the great myths of creation told by many tribes.

Wherever a sun-catching myth is found the characters vary with the locality. Sometimes the sun catcher is the Trickster-Hero in his heroic capacity. Sometimes, as in this instance, it is one of the lowliest of creatures. In this instance, too, we find that even a great myth may contain "how and why" elements.

▼▼▼▼▼▼

There was no light anywhere, and the animal people stumbled around in the darkness. Whenever one bumped into another, he would say, "What we need in the world is light." And the other would reply, "Yes, indeed, light is what we badly need."

At last, the animals called a meeting, and gathered together as well as they could in the dark. The red-headed woodpecker said, "I have heard that over on the other side of the world there are people who have light."

"Good, good!" said everyone.

"Perhaps if we go over there, they will give us some light," the woodpecker suggested.

"If they have all the light there is," the fox said, "they must be greedy people, who would not want to give any of it up. Maybe we should just go over there and take the light from them."

"Who shall go?" cried everyone, and the animals all began talking at once, arguing about who was strongest and ran fastest, who was best able to go and get the light.

Finally the 'possum said, "I can try. I have a fine big bushy tail, and I can hide the light inside my fur."

"Good! Good!" said all the others, and the 'possum set out.

As he traveled eastward, the light began to grow and grow, until it dazzled his eyes, and the 'possum screwed his eyes up to keep out the bright light. Even today, if you notice, you will see that the 'possum's eyes are almost shut, and that he comes out of his house only at night.

All the same, the 'possum kept going, clear to the other side of the world, and there he found the sun. He snatched a little piece of it and hid it in the fur of his fine bushy tail, but the sun was so hot it burned off all the fur, and by the time the 'possum got home his tail was as bare as it is today.

"Oh, dear!" everyone said. "Our brother has lost his fine bushy tail, and still we have no light."

"I'll go," said the buzzard. "I have better sense than to put the sun on my tail. I'll put it on my head."

So the buzzard traveled eastward till he came to the place where the sun was. And because the buzzard flies so high, the sun-keeping people did not see him, although now they were watching out for thieves. The buzzard dived straight down out of the sky, the way he does today, and caught a piece of the sun in his claws. He set the sun on his head and started for home, but the sun was so hot that it burned off all his head feathers, and that is why the buzzard's head is bald today.

Now the people were in despair. "What shall we do? What shall we do?" they cried. "Our brothers have tried hard; they have done their best, everything a man can do. What else shall we do so we can have light?"

"They have done the best a man can do," said a little voice from the grass, "but perhaps this is something a woman can do better than a man."

"Who are you?" everyone asked. "Who is that speaking in a tiny voice and hidden in the grass?"

"I am your Grandmother Spider," she replied. "Perhaps I was put in the world to bring you light. Who knows? At least I can try, and if I am burned up it will still not be as if you had lost one of your great warriors."

Then Grandmother Spider felt around her in the darkness until she found some damp clay. She rolled it in her hands, and molded a little clay bowl. She started eastward, carrying her bowl, and spinning a thread behind her so she could find her way back.

When Grandmother Spider came to the place of the sun people, she was so little and so quiet no one noticed her. She reached out gently, gently, and took a tiny bit of the sun, and placed it in her clay bowl. Then she went back along the thread that she had spun, with the sun's light growing and spreading before her, as she moved from east to west. And if you will notice, even today a spider's web is shaped like the sun's disk and its rays, and the spider will always spin her web in the morning, very early, before the sun is fully up.

"Thank you, Grandmother," the people said when she returned. "We will always honor you and we will always remember you."

And from then on pottery making became woman's work, and all pottery must be dried slowly in the shade before it is put in the heat of the firing oven, just as Grandmother Spider's bowl dried in her hand, slowly, in the darkness, as she traveled toward the land of the sun.

▼▼▼▼▼

From: Kilpatrick, Jack Frederick, and Kilpatrick, Anna Gritts, Eastern Cherokee Folktales. *Bureau of American Ethnology, Anthropological Papers 75–80, Bulletin 196, pp. 379–448. Washington, D.C.: Government Printing Office, 1966.*

The Sky Beings:
Thunder and His Helpers

The history of the League of the Iroquois is inextricably tangled with the history of the United States. Apparently this union of Five Nations—the Cayuga, Mohawk, Oneida, Onondaga, and Seneca—who spoke mutually intelligible languages, began after the first European landings in eastern North America. Its organization became one of the models for the United States Constitution.

From the west, where the Seneca held Lake Erie, to the Atlantic coast, where the Mohawk were settled, the "Long House" of the Five Nations extended its control over other Indian groups, many of whom spoke languages unrelated to Iroquois.

The Indians of the Five Nations were partly horticultural, partly hunting and fishing peoples. All used canoes, birchbark in the north and log dugouts in the south. Maize, beans, squash, and tobacco were their principal crops, with the tobacco planted in separate gardens from the vegetables.

Iroquoian peoples made fine pottery, but also used bowls and spoons carved from wood. They had some knowledge of working copper, and

33

made ornaments from that metal, but did not develop metal tools before the white conquest. Birchbark containers, sometimes with designs bitten into the surface of the bark, sometimes with cut-out decorations, were used for maple sugar, wild rice, dried meat and fish, and storage of clothing.

The Iroquois must have possessed a rich mythology, although only fragments of it have survived. Like their linguistic relatives, the southern Cherokee, the northern Iroquois regarded Thunder and his sky relatives as having great supernatural power. Most of the surviving Iroquoian myths are concerned with thunder, rain, the clouds, and their helpfulness to man. These good characters are opposed, in Iroquoian mythology, by a swarm of evil underwater monsters, or snakes.

Today, some Iroquois live in northern New York State, and a few removed groups are settled in northeastern Oklahoma, near the Cherokees. In each group, some of the old ceremonies are still performed, old songs are sung, and a few legends survive.

Similar stories with similar characters are told by the Cherokees. They are also told by the Creeks, who lived south of the Cherokees before removal to Oklahoma, and have been reported from the Natchez, who were south of the Creeks, and from the Yuchi, to the west. The Pawnees, on the eastern margin of the plains, may have possessed a similar legend for they, too, do not break ground for planting until after the first spring thunder. Apparently the ideas of the myths were well-distributed between the Atlantic seaboard and the Mississippi-Great Lakes drainage.

▼▼▼▼▼▼

Once, long ago, three young men went hunting together. They were brother-friends, who had promised to care for each other's lives as if each were his own.

The three brother-friends were far from home when one of them tripped on a twisted root, and fell heavily to the ground. His leg was bent back under him, and when his friends lifted him up they saw that it was broken.

"Don't leave me, my friends," the injured man begged. "You know what we have promised each other. Help me to get home to my mother, for she has no one else to take care of her."

So the two young men who weren't hurt helped him. They made splints of saplings, and bound them around the broken leg with vines. They covered his whole leg with rawhide, and between them helped their friend start for home.

As they went on, the lame man grew heavier and heavier on his friends' shoulders. They stopped sometimes and laid him down so he could rest. When the three started on, the two who were not hurt changed sides so the balance would not be destroyed. Each time the three men stopped, the two who were not hurt were more tired. They looked at each other over their injured friend's head, and with their eyes, the two agreed to a plan.

At last, as they trudged along a high ridge, the three came to a deep ravine. There the two who were not hurt took hold of their brother-friend, and swung him up in the air, over the edge of the ravine, and dropped him. Quickly, the two men turned away and hurried home. They entered the village with tears streaming down their faces, weeping and mourning.

"What has happened? What has happened?" all the people in the village cried out, as they came running to meet the returning hunters.

"Oh, our poor friend!" they wailed. "As we went through the woods, an enemy attacked us. We fought them off, but a last stray arrow struck our brother, and he is dead."

"Oh, my son! My son!" wept his mother. "I am alone in my old age, with no one to care for me. How can I live without my poor boy?"

"That's all right, mother," his friends said, "we'll take care of you."

"How can I rest?" the mother mourned. "If he had died at home his clansmen would have buried him, and I would know his soul was safe!"

"Don't worry about that," the friends assured her. "We buried him deep and safe. No ugly spirits can reach him, and no wild animals can dig him up."

The mother was a little comforted then. As time went on, she stopped mourning outwardly, although her heart was always hurting for her boy.

The young man fell to the bottom of the crevice in the mountains, where his friends had dropped him, and lay there unconscious for many hours. When he opened his eyes, he saw an old man sitting beside him. The old man's long gray hair hung loose on his shoulders, and his scalp lock had grown out to the same length as the rest.

Behind him there was a cave in the side of the ravine. There was something strange about that old man. The hunter did not know what it was.

"Who are you?" the young man asked.

"I live here," the old man answered him, without giving his name. "This is my home. How did you come here? You could not have walked, with a broken leg."

"My friends dropped me over the edge," the young man replied. "How could they treat me like that? I trusted them; we were like brothers to each other! How can I get home? Who will take care of my mother? They threw me away to die."

"Stay here with me and do what I tell you, and you won't die," said the old man. "If you obey me, you will be all right."

"What do you want me to do?" the young man asked.

"I need someone to hunt for me," the old man told him. "I am too old to go out and hunt for myself. I can cure you, and when I do, you must promise to stay here and bring me whatever game you kill. I will save your life, but you must take care of me in return."

"I promise," said the young man.

The old man went away, and when he came back he brought a bowl full of water, and another one full of herbs. He soaked the herbs in the water while he cut off the bandage and drew the splints away from the injured leg. Then the old man bound herb compresses over the injury, and soon the leg began to heal.

By fall, the young man was well again, and he went out hunting every day. Usually he found only enough game to carry home himself, but sometimes he killed a deer or elk which was too much for one man to load and carry. Then the old man came out and helped the young one, and they brought the game in together. The hunter never tried to climb the walls of the ravine where the cave was hidden.

The young man hunted all winter. Then it was spring. The warm winds blew, and soft showers fell. Animals that had been in hiding all winter came out of their dens, and the hunting was better than it had been in the cold weather. The young man wondered what life was like outside the ravine.

One day the young man saw huge footprints on the ground. He tracked them, up the canyon walls, across the flats, to the edge of the deep woods, and came upon a black bear—the biggest he had ever seen. The bear did not see the man, and the hunter killed him with a single arrow, right in the heart.

As he bent over to feel the bear's fatness and guess its weight, the young man heard voices speaking behind him. He had never met anyone on his earlier hunting trips, but now he was outside the ravine. He

turned and saw four men, dressed in strange, cloudlike robes, standing behind him, watching him.

"Who are you?" the young man asked.

"We are the Thunders," the four cloud-figures answered. "We
were put here on earth to help everybody—all the people—whoever is
in need. We are supposed to keep order in the world. If there is
drought, we bring rain. If there are cruel people or mean animals, we
destroy them. Now we are looking for the old man who lives in the
deep ravine, for he is a very bad man."

"I work for him," the hunter said. "I killed this bear for him. He
saved my life, so whatever he tells me to do, I must do."

"Are you happy with this life?" the Thunders asked.

"No," answered the young man. "I want to go back to my own
people. My mother needs me."

"If you will help us against the old man who is taking all your
food and turning you as thin as an eel in the springtime, we will take
you home," said the Thunders. "That is part of our work, to keep the
people well and happy."

"I will help you," the young man promised.

"Then do as we tell you," the Thunders directed him. "Go back
to the old man and tell him you have killed a bear. Tell him it is too
heavy for you to carry alone, and ask him to help you bring it in."

The young man did as the Thunders told him. The old man was
angry because his servant had left the ravine, but was delighted when
he heard there would be fat bear meat. He took his stone knife, sharp-
ened as keen as it could be, to cut up the bear. They started off, with
the old man hurrying ahead of the young one, in his eagerness to
reach the game.

"There it is! I see it!" he cried as they came upon the black
furry mound.

The two men went to work, and soon the bear was skinned and cut
up, ready to take home.

"Put it all on my shoulders," the old man ordered, and when the
young man hesitated because he did not think the old one could carry
such a load, he insisted, "More! More! Pile it on! I can hardly wait to
get home to eat some of that fat meat!"

It was getting late now, and the sky was getting darker.

"Do you think it will rain? Do you see any clouds?" the old man
asked. He was bent over under the burden he insisted on carrying.

"No, it's all clear," the young man assured him, and they started
home.

"Let me know if you see even a tiny cloud," the old man ordered,
and the young man said, "All right."

Soon there was a cloud to the northeast, but the young man didn't say anything. The cloud grew nearer and nearer and larger and larger, until it stopped before them and the Thunders stepped out of its folds. The old man dropped his load and started to run away. He turned himself into a giant porcupine, and shot poisoned quills backward at his enemies. But the Thunders turned the quills aside with their power and followed him, throwing lightning bolts ahead of them. Just as the old man porcupine reached his cave the lightning struck him, and he fell to the ground dead.

"Now we have finished our work here," the Thunders said. "That old man made slaves of everybody, until he wore them out and killed them."

"Thank you, thank you!" the young man exclaimed. "How can I ever show you how grateful I am?"

"Perhaps some day you will do something for us," the Thunders assured him. "A time will come when you can make your return. Now, hurry, because your mother is still grieving for you."

They gave the young man a cloud robe like theirs to wear, and showed him how to move the wings fastened to its shoulders. The young man hurried home, and came down in his mother's corn field late at night. He took off his cloud robe and hid it away, and then ran to the house. He drew aside the mat over the door of the little bark house where his mother lived all alone.

The mother was sitting there, combing her hair before she went to bed. She looked up and saw her son standing in the door, and she was frightened. "Who are you? What are you doing here? I have done nothing wrong; no ghost should come after me!" she cried.

"Don't be frightened, Mother," he reassured her. "It really is I, your son, and not a ghost at all."

"Come in," said the mother, and held out her arms to him as if he were a little boy again. And so they hugged each other and cried together with happiness because they were united once more.

Next morning the Thunders came to see that all was well. When they saw how happy the young man and his mother were, the Thunders were much pleased. "That's good, that's the way we like to see good people live," they said. "Then we know we have done what we were sent to earth to do. Do right to every one, and you will be happy always."

"Are you going to leave us?" the young man cried.

"Our work is finished for this year," said the Thunders. "We will be back again, many times. Keep the cloud robe, and when we come again you can travel with us, and perhaps help us with our work."

The young man and his mother hid the cloud robe away. The mother took care of the garden, and the young man hunted and fished. They lived well, and were happy and prosperous. When people in the village asked the young man where he had been, he only told them that he had been away and had come back. He would not say even one unkind thing about his friends.

In the spring, the Thunders returned. "Come and fly with us, friend," they said.

The young man took out his cloud robe and put it on. Then he and the Thunders flew above the earth, watching for people who were wronged or unhappy, and putting things right for them again. Sometimes the fliers dipped down to the earth and drank from ponds and streams. Sometimes they soared high in the sky until the earth was only a speck below them. But they always knew where they were needed, and those were the places where they alighted.

"We are looking for our enemies," the Thunders said. "There is one more, who does great harm to mankind. When we find and destroy him, then everything will be all right."

One day the young man dropped down to earth and drank from a pool he had seen from the air. When he rose again and rejoined the Thunders, they saw that his lips were coated with something shiny, like oil.

"What is that?" the Thunders asked. "How did you get that shine on your mouth?"

"I drank from that little pool down there," the young man said, and he showed the Thunders which pool it was.

"That is the place we have been looking for!" the Thunders exclaimed. "That's the pool where our enemy lives. We would never have found it except for the oil he puts out, which coated your lips. Now, you see, you have made your return. You found our enemy for us."

The Thunders all worked together. They made a great bolt of lightning and hurled it into the pool. The lightning was so strong it blasted the pool open, and in the bottom of it there was a great grub, like the cutworms that chew down young plants in the gardens, but a thousand thousand times as big.

"He's dead!" cried the young man.

"Yes," said the Thunders. "From now on, the spring lightning will kill all the grubs in your gardens. If people will turn the earth in the spring so the lightning can get to it, we will make it clean. Go home now, and tell your people this."

The young man hurried home to take the message to all the people. From that time on, the people honored the Thunders, and respected

them, and they never broke ground until after the first Thunder came
in the spring.

▼▼▼▼▼▼

As told to Alice Marriott by Malinda Peacock, Seneca.
Also recorded in Smith, Erminie A., Myths of the Iroquois. *Bureau of
    Ethnology Annual Report No. 2, 1880–1881, pp. 51–122. Wash-
    ington D.C.: Government Printing Office, 1883.*

The Waters Beneath:
Fifty Young Men
and a Turtle

Every stream and pool in the Cheyenne country in Montana and Wyoming has water-monster stories of this sort. In this instance the myth has been transferred to an Oklahoma setting.

Out on the High Plains, near Canton, Oklahoma, there is a pit, a hole in the ground. Scientists go there from the University to dig bones out of the pit and study them. The geologists say that the bones are those of animals who died out long ago, but the Cheyennes know better. Cheyennes hunted the High Plains long before the white men came, and they know how those bones came to be there. This is the Cheyenne story.

They say that one time, long ago, fifty young men who belonged to the same warrior society set out to go buffalo hunting. That was long before even the Cheyenne had horses or guns or iron knives. The young men traveled on foot, and they took with them their stone-headed axes and their stone-bladed spears. They hung extra moccasins around their necks by braiding the tie strings together until each man had a wreath of moccasins hanging around his shoulders.

The young men started at the edge of the Cross Timbers, in the middle of Oklahoma, and journeyed to the west as far as the high mountains where the people go to cut their tipi poles. Nowhere in all that country did the young men find any enemies: no Utes, no Navahos, no Apaches, nobody. At last the party gave up and started home. The leader said, ''We will start hunting when we are four days out from our home camp.''

They came down the last slopes of the mountains and crossed the barren Staked Plains, where the Comanches marked the trails from one water hole to the next with stubs of yucca thrust into the ground, so no one would die of thirst in the crossing. Oh, they are desolate, those Staked Plains! Nothing but rolling land as far as you can see, until you come to a place where the ground breaks and falls away, down, into a canyon. You can see a mirage shining like water on the ground, always just ahead of you as you travel, and it is hard not to leave the marked trail and run into the mirage and splash around in the make-believe water.

That is why, when the young men saw something shining on the ground ahead of them, they were not surprised. The track led toward the shining thing. It could not be a mirage, because as the young men walked they drew nearer and nearer to the shining thing, and it grew bigger in their eyes, shining and glowing like a hill of glass, and reflecting the sun back like a mirror. They all stopped to look at the wonderful sight.

''Let's go over there and see what that is,'' said some of the young men.

Others said, ''No! That is something mysterious and it may be dangerous. Let us travel the other way.''

''The marked trail leads toward it,'' the chief said finally. ''We must follow the stakes to find water. If that is something wonderful that is meant for us, it will be right on the trail.''

They followed the yucca stakes all morning, and at noon they stood beside the shining object. Then the young men were more amazed than ever, for they saw that it was a great water turtle with a shining shell, and that the turtle walked slowly along the ground, following the staked trail to the water hole as if it were a person.

''Where do you think he's going?'' one young man asked, but no one could answer him, for nobody knew where the turtle was traveling.

"I'm going to go for a ride on his back," said the young man, foolishly. He climbed on the turtle's back, and the turtle carried him, slowly, slowly as it crawled along the trail.

"My, he's strong!" another young man said. He, too, climbed on the turtle's back, and the turtle carried both friends slowly forward, moving steadily to the east as it went.

One after another, forty-nine of the young men climbed on the turtle's back, until at last only their chief was left walking beside the turtle.

"I wonder what makes him so strong," said the first young man to ride the turtle. "I'm going to see his muscles if I can." And he took the point of his spear, and tried to pry the turtle's shells apart. The others imitated him. The turtle gave no sign that it was hurt; the shells remained tight together, and the great creature still carried its load forward.

"Get down," the chief of the war party ordered his friends. "We can walk beside him and keep him company as long as he follows the trail, but he is too powerful to play with, or to try to hurt. Get down, and walk with me."

The young men on the turtle's back began to argue among themselves. Some thought the turtle was a mystery that had been sent to them, and that they should all stay with him. Others thought the turtle had dangerous power, and they should leave him alone. These last young men tried to get off the turtle to walk. When they did so, the young men found that they were stuck tight to the turtle's back.

When the young men found that they could not get away from the turtle, they began to attack it with their stone-headed axes and spears. The young men hit the turtle on the head, and tried to beat it so that it would stop. But the spear-points splintered against the turtle's shell, and the ax heads stuck to the turtle's head, and all their weapons were useless.

Then the forty-nine young men cried out to their leader, "Save us! Help us! You are the chief of our war party; it is up to you to save us from this thing!"

"Stop, please stop," the chief said to the turtle. "Let my brothers get down, and we will wait here until you have gone on your way. They are sorry they tried to hurt you. Forgive them and be merciful, because you are stronger than they are. Let those poor young men go free, and they will honor you forever. They will dance the Sun Dance for you."

But the turtle crawled steadily forward, and the young men could not get off his back.

The chief of the war party ran beside the turtle, weeping and pleading, but the turtle crawled on, and the young men could not get free.

Their shadows lengthened before them, for the day was drawing in to its close. Ahead, the chief could see a pool of water, not shining in the sunset, but lying dead and dull in a hollow of the prairies. The turtle was heading straight for the lake.

The young men on the turtle's back saw the lake, too. Then they truly were frightened. They all began to pray and cry for mercy, but the turtle ignored them all, and went straight ahead, along the line of yucca stakes, to the lake where the trail ended.

"Stop!" the chief begged him. "Let my foolish friends get down. Show us your strength through your mercy."

But still the turtle crawled forward.

"I have done all I can do," the chief said to his friends. "Something wonderful was shown to you, and you did not respect it. Now you will be punished because you thought wrong in your hearts. I cannot change anything."

"Go home," said the young men as the turtle carried them along to the lake. "That's all you can do, go home. Tell the people what happened. Tell our families we love them and we will mourn for them. They should mourn for us, too."

"That's all I can do," said the chief. He raised his arm in farewell. "I will tell the people what happened, and that they must mourn for you."

His friends raised their arms, too, as the turtle stepped into the lake. The forty-nine young men waved to their chief.

"Go back," they begged him, "and tell our sisters what happened. Bring them here this time next year, so they can mourn for us on this spot."

To the last minute, as the turtle carried them down, down into the water, the young men waved to their chief, and begged him to bring the mourners back the next year. Weeping and sighing, the chief promised his friends that he would do what they asked.

When the chief came home alone and empty-handed, all the people in camp came running out to meet him. "Where are our sons? Where are our brothers?" they cried. "There must have been a great battle if they all are killed and you are left alone! Tell us what happened."

"There was no battle," the chief said sorrowfully. "They were carried away by something mysterious and powerful. Listen, and I will tell you what happened." And he began to tell, and as he told, the people wept and mourned more dismally than ever.

When the chief had finished speaking, the people said, "We will all go with you next year in the spring, and we will mourn by the lake, as our sons and brothers begged us to."

In spring, when the grass was thick and stood as high as a horse's hocks, and there was standing water everywhere, the whole village set out. They traveled westward to the edge of the Staked Plains, and there the chief of the young men picked up the marked trail that led on, still to the west, to the lake where his friends were lost.

The chief did not find the lake. Instead, he came to a place where a great lake once had been. In the middle of the old lake bed there was a deep hole, going down, down into the earth, and that hole was filled with bones. The lake bed and the bones still are there.

Then all the people set down their loads around the dry lake shore and mourned there, for they knew that the bones were those of the forty-nine young men the turtle had carried into the water. That happened a long time ago, so the old people say.

▼▼▼▼▼

Told to Alice Marriott by Mary Little Bear Inkanish.

The Waters Beneath:
The Underwater Village

KIOWA

The Kiowas are as characteristic of the southern plains as the Cheyennes are of the northern. No one knows for certain the point of origin and earliest territory of the Kiowas. A Spanish source places them on the Yellowstone River about 1706. Probably the group went that far north only occasionally, for all other early written records place the Kiowas in or near their present homeland in southwestern Oklahoma.

Kiowa material culture is as streamlined as Cheyenne is elaborate. The porcupine did not live in the Kiowa country, and, in any case, it was an animal protected by a religious tabu. Its flesh could not be eaten or its quills drawn. The Kiowas therefore used painted designs instead of quill embroidery. Very early, too, through their contacts with Mexican traders, the Kiowas learned to work in metal, and in 1842 Randolph Marcy, running a War Department survey on the Red River, identified a group of Kiowa horsemen at a distance by "the flash of their silver bridles and ornaments in the sun." It was not until twenty-five years later the first crude, fumbling attempts at metalwork were made by the Navahos.

Throughout their written history the Kiowas have been associated with the Kiowa-Apaches. The source of this alliance is as lost as the source of either group. The Kiowa-Apaches are Athabascan-speaking;

46

the Kiowa language is only faintly, if at all, related to any other. Although their relationship was symbiotic in warfare and ceremonialism, the two groups preserved not only their linguistic identities, but social, governmental, and religious distinctions, in spite of identical material cultures.

The lake described in the following story cannot be identified as positively as can the shiny mountains and the pool of bones of the Cheyenne legend. The drowned-village theme is less usual in the plains than it is in other areas. In fact, the description of it in this story is a little like the Breton tale of la cathédrale engloutie, *although it is highly unlikely that the informant who told the story knew anything of European folklore at the time of telling.*

Possibly this is a fragment, or combination of fragments, of a longer and more complex story. However, it can stand by itself. The introduction of smallpox as a threat and a terror occurs in other, briefer stories, but this version is used here as an illustration of the combinations of myths that can occur. In this case the water becomes a beneficent and protective power.

▼▼▼▼▼▼

Once, they say, a young man left his family at home in his village and went out hunting. He killed a fine fat deer, and skinned it out. As he was coming home with the bundle of meat tied up in the deer hide on his back, he met a rather elderly man.

The hunter was frightened when he saw the stranger. The older man's lips were swollen. His eyes were swollen almost shut. His body was covered with open running sores. A terrible smell filled the air around him.

"Who are you?" the hunter cried out. "Where do you come from and where are you going?"

"I am Smallpox," the visitor answered, and the smell of his breath was worse than the smell of his body. "I come from the east, where the white people are, and I am going to the west to find the Indians. When you leave here I will follow your trail to your village."

"Why do you want to do that?" the hunter exclaimed. "The Indians haven't hurt you. They haven't hurt the white people, either, if it comes to that. They never even heard of them. Why do you want to be cruel to the Indians?"

"I'm coming," Smallpox answered. "It was willed for me to

come. I am going to that camp over there and give everyone my disease because that is what was willed.''

''Don't do that!'' the hunter protested. ''There are good people in that camp. Be pitiful to them, don't hurt them. We haven't done you any harm.''

For a long time Smallpox stood and thought. At last he said, ''Very well. I will have pity on you. You can take your family, and as many of your friends as you like. If you want, you can take the whole camp. If they will follow you, they will be all right. It is willed for you to lead them to a safe place. Go home and get your family, and then leave. Go in the opposite direction. Get clear away.''

The hunter went home to his village. He sent for the crier, and told him to call the people together. When everyone had assembled, the hunter made his announcement.

''Something is coming,'' he told the people. ''A terrible thing is going to happen. There is sickness coming that could kill us all. But it has been willed that I can lead my family and friends away from it. Follow me, and you will live; you will not die.''

He was a young man, who had never led a war party, and the people were surprised to hear him talk like that. They listened for a while, and then they began to laugh.

''Oh, it's no such thing!'' the old men said. ''Nothing is going to happen. You don't have to pay attention to him, all you people. Everything will be all right.''

''I was sent with a warning,'' the hunter insisted. ''Something bad is going to happen to everyone who does not follow me.''

But still the people laughed, and refused to believe him. The old men said the hunter was a liar, and no good. ''He's never done anything to make you believe him,'' they said.

At last the hunter gave up. ''Stay here, if you like. I will obey the power,'' he announced, and went home to his tipi.

That night, while all the village was asleep, the hunter and his family got up and packed their belongings. He did this although he knew that when the village woke in the morning the people would say, ''That man is a coward. There's nothing for anybody to be afraid of.''

The family left the village and traveled westward across the short grass of the High Plains. On and on and on they went. Finally the family came to a great body of water. It was deep and clear and blue. It looked fierce. Perhaps that lake is still there, somewhere. People say that it is.

Whatever spirit it was that had warned the hunter took his hand, and drew him and his family under the water. That was the last that anyone heard from them for many, many years. All the people who stayed behind in the camp were wiped out, as soon as Smallpox spoke to them and they smelled his terrible breath.

Many years later, two young men went out. They weren't hunting, they weren't fighting, perhaps they were looking for women. Probably the young men didn't much care whether they found new wives or not. They must have felt that if they did find women, it would be good to take their wives home. It was all right with them.

As the two friends traveled, they came to the deep, blue, fierce lake. On the east side the wanderers saw a track, going into the water, that looked as if tipi poles had been dragged along the ground in that place. They wondered about it. Then they walked around the lake to the west side, and looked for the place where the drags came out of the water. They couldn't find it.

"Well, it's getting dark," the older of the two said. "Let's go to sleep, and we can search again in the morning. If people went into the water, they must have come out. Their camp can't be very far away. Those were fresh tracks. We'll find them tomorrow."

The two young men ate some mesquite meal and dried meat, and washed their food down with water from the lake. Then the two friends rolled up in their buffalo robes and lay down to sleep on the west side of the lake.

It was a clear, bright night. When the stars were standing still above him, the older man wakened, and shook his friend's shoulder.

"Listen," he said in a whisper. "Tell me. Do you hear anything?"

They both listened, and they both heard it. There was the sound of a drum, and of singing, coming from the bottom of the lake.

"Who is that?" asked the younger friend.

The older one thought about it. Then he remembered what his grandfather had told him about the people who left before Smallpox came. "It's the people who went away," he answered. "It must be their village there, down in the water."

"In the morning we'll go and find them," said his friend.

"Yes," the older one agreed, "in the morning we'll go and find them and take them home with us."

But when morning came and the young men searched the shore of the lake, they still could find only the one track leading down into the water. They walked along it to the edge, but then they were afraid, and turned back.

"Let's go home," said the elder traveler. "We can ask the old people what they think."

"That's good," replied his friend, and they started back to their own village.

All their friends came out to meet the young men, and listened attentively to the story that they told.

"Let's all go there," said the band chief. "We can try to find our brothers under the water." So they all started back with the young men.

When the people of the village reached the lake, they went around its shores, looking everywhere for tracks. Always they came back to the same place on the east side, where the tipi poles had been dragged down under the water. Nowhere could even the most skillful trackers find a place where the village left the lake.

"How can we see our brothers?" the village chief asked the old men. "How can we reach them, to let them know that we are here?"

And the old men shook their heads and mourned, and answered the chief, "There is no way that we can join them unless we have magic. We must have wonderful power to go down under the water and to live there. Without that power, we will all be drowned."

But they all went back, again and yet again, to the place where the tipi poles had been dragged under the water, and the tracks of the people had just been wiped out. When they sat and listened in the nighttime, people could hear the drums and the singing; could hear men talking and women laughing and children playing, there in the drowned village in the bottom of the lake.

For many years after that the Kiowa-Apaches—for all the people in this story were Kiowa-Apaches—used to visit the lake. When they came home, the people would dance, and sing the song of the man who led the village under the water:

> "The world is a dangerous place
> For the Indians to live.
> Come with me, my people,
> And I will lead you to safety.
> There, under the water, there
> Is a magical place.
> It is a place created
> To keep the Indians safe."

▼▼▼▼▼

As told to Ioleta MacElhaney and Alice Marriott by Eagle Plume (Frank Givens). Translated by Ioleta MacElhaney.

The Waters Beneath:
The Great River Monster

▼▼▼▼▼▼▼▼▼▼▼▼▼▼▼▼▼▼▼▼▼▼▼▼▼▼▼▼▼▼▼▼ CHEYENNE

The story of the monster who lives in the Mississippi River must be older than any recorded North American history.

Temple mounds and isolated burials alike, the length of the river, contain carved stone effigies of the plumed (or horned) serpent. His likeness is engraved on pottery and shaped in shell and wood. He is as omnipresent in the Mississippi drainage as in the central valley of Mexico. A plumed water serpent is also venerated by the village Indians who live from the Rio Grande Valley westward into central Arizona.

The story that follows is an explanation of a contemporary Cheyenne custom, that of making an offering of food or tobacco whenever one crosses a large body of water, or stands beside a lake or ocean. This sacrifice, too, is of prewhite origin, and the offerings keep their original form.

▼▼▼▼▼▼

Two young men went off traveling, to see the country. They walked a long way, and became very hungry. They couldn't find anything to

51

eat, and at last the friends were so tired that they sat down and rested, to get strength to go on.

One day, the young men had traveled a long way. They came out on the high prairie, where there was nothing in sight but the grass, bending to the wind as if it were dancing. Suddenly, the travelers found two great big eggs, just lying there on the ground.

"Come here," one young man called to the other. "I have found a blessing. We have been hungry, and here is food for us to eat. Look at these big eggs. They will make a whole meal for both of us."

"No," said his friend, "I don't think we should eat something magical like that. It might be dangerous for us, and do us harm. Those eggs are too big to be real, and I don't want to eat them."

"What if they are big?" asked the first youth. "That means a bigger blessing. Perhaps some bird or turtle we never even saw laid those eggs, and I know they are safe to eat."

The one who had found the eggs built a fire of buffalo chips, and roasted the eggs beside it, turning them and turning them until they were done. "Here," he told his friend, "see how good they are. Eat one." And he popped the shell off his own egg and began to eat it greedily. "It's just right inside," said the young man, "just the way you like it. Come on. Eat it." But still the friend refused, so the greedy young man not only ate his own egg, he ate most of the second one.

After the young men had rested a while, they started on. Then the one who ate the eggs began to feel sick. He staggered when he walked; he stumbled over the tufts of grass. But there was nowhere to stop, and they went on until it was dark. Then the young men stopped and camped out there on the open prairie.

In the morning, the greedy young man wakened his friend.

"Get up and help me," he begged. "I feel as if I couldn't walk. My legs are heavy, and so stiff I can hardly move them. I don't know what's the matter."

"Let me see," said his friend. "Perhaps there is something I can do to help." He drew off his friend's moccasins, and saw that the young man's legs were no longer smooth and brown. The skin was striped and scaly, like a snake's hide.

"Let's go on," said the sick man. "Perhaps we can find water. If I could only have water to drink, perhaps I would feel better."

The young men started on, but the one who was sick could hardly walk. His legs were so heavy they dragged him back, and every now and then he had to stop to rest. At last his legs became so heavy that he had to crawl along the ground, dragging them behind him.

"Don't leave me, my friend," the young man begged. "I will never live if you leave me here alone. We've always been together, since we were little boys, and we've always loved each other. Please don't leave me."

"I won't leave you," his friend promised. "I will stay with you until you are safe. I promise."

At nightfall they came to a little lake. "Let's camp here and rest," the sick one said. "Perhaps if I go swimming it will make me feel better. I feel that if my legs are wet, I will rest better."

"You go while I make a fire," said the friend.

So the first young man went into the lake, and swam and dived, into the water and on the water, leaping and twisting his whole body when he moved. "I feel well, now," he called to his friend, "better than I ever did before in all my life."

"Come out and rest now," the friend answered. "Don't get too tired."

"All right," said the sick man, and he dragged himself out of the water, onto the shore of the lake. His legs were joined together, and the whole lower part of his body was a snake's.

That night they rested beside the lake, and in the morning the young men went on, looking for their home camp.

"Take me home," the sick one pleaded. "There's somewhere that I have to go. Take me home."

So they went on, slowly, slowly all the day long, and at nightfall they came to another lake.

"This is not the place I am looking for yet," said the snake-man, "but it will do to rest. Help me into the water, and I will stay there tonight."

All night long the friend sat beside the lake, and listened to the snake-man splashing and leaping in the water, and waited for daylight. At last the east turned white and the snake-man came out of the water. Only his arms and his head were a man's now. The rest was all snake.

"Let's go on," the snake-man said to his friend. By now he could hardly speak, and his words were whistles and gasps. "I know now where I am to go. They are calling me to come to the Mississippi River. Help me to get there, and I will be all right."

So they went on again, all day, with the friend walking beside the snake. Now his body stretched out, and he left a great snake's trail behind him in the dust. All day long the snake begged his friend not to leave him until he came to the end of his road.

Late in the evening, when it was almost dark, the two friends reached the Mississippi River. "This is where I am to go," the snake-man said. "Stay with me a little longer, brother, because there is something else for you to know. Don't go back until I tell you to, but when you go, don't mourn for me. From now on I will be all right." And he slithered down the bank and sank into the muddy water and disappeared.

His friend paced the bank, crying and praying, most of the night. Near daylight, he fell asleep. He was wakened by a voice that spoke to him.

"My friend, my friend," it called. "Wake up! Wake up, and look at me!"

The young man stared at the river. Rising from it was a great snake. His body was covered with bluish skin, he had twin horns on his head, and there was a little red dot under each of his eyes.

"My brother," he said, "don't be afraid. It's only I."

"No," said the brother-friend. "I still love you, and I am not afraid."

"Well, my friend," said the snake-man, "they sent for me here. This where I belong to be. From now on, I will lie here in the middle of the riverbed, and will fill it from side to side. My body will stretch out as long as the Mississippi. Go back, and tell my friends not to worry about me.

"You must tell them something else, too," the snake-man went on. "Tell them I'm not dead, I'm taking care of the river. Whenever you cross, you must bring a buffalo paunch, or some of the other inside meats, and drop them in the middle of the river for me to eat. Or you can drop tobacco in for me to smoke. Whenever anybody does that, I will give him my blessing."

"I will tell the people," his brother-friend said. "I will tell all your relatives."

"You can tell them," the snake-man replied, "but tell my relatives not to try to come to see me. If they do, it won't be very good for them."

"I'll be sure to tell them that," his friend said.

"Come to me," the snake-man said. "I want to kiss you good-by, because we shall never meet again on this earth. Don't be afraid; I won't hurt you."

So the young man put his arms around his friend, and the snake licked his face with his forked tongue, and told him never to forget.

Then the young man went back, alone, to the village, and told the story.

"Take us there," the snake-man's parents entreated him. "Take us where we can see our son."

At first the young man refused, but the parents begged so hard that at last, against his better judgment, he agreed to take them. "I don't want to do it," he warned them. "Something bad could happen if you go."

When they reached the river bank, they saw that it was covered with great waves, and that there was fire rising up from the place where their son had disappeared. It was a warning, and the parents turned back and went home, sorrowfully.

Ever since, when Cheyennes cross a main body of water, they take food and tobacco with them, to drop in as a present to the snake-man and his underwater relatives.

▼▼▼▼▼

Told to Alice Marriott and Carol K. Rachlin by Mary Little Bear Inkanish.

The Stars Above:
Pursuit of the Bear

Hunters, fishermen, farmers—all people who make their livings from the land or sea—must be aware of weather, seasons, and the stars. Every productive activity is directly controlled by nature, and such people know that fact.

The great ceremonies of the North American Indians were seasonal. Some were based on the solstices and equinoxes; others were determined by the positions of certain stars or groups of stars in the sky.

Much North American Indian star lore has been lost, for several reasons. First, determination of ceremonies was dependent on secret knowledge, revealed only to the priests, and told by them only to men they trained to succeed them. Second, many constellations known to Indians did not have European equivalents. Third, many of the earliest recorders who worked with Indians were city people, unfamiliar with the astronomy of their own culture.

The Musquakie (Yellow Earth People), or Fox, with their allies the Sauk (Red Earth People), were among the Algonkian-speaking Indian groups who were pushed westward by the combination of European invasion and Iroquoian aggression.

56

On their own land, chosen for its fertility and nearness to streams, the Fox set up a village of mat-covered, vaulted wigwams, with bark houses for summer use, surrounded by corn fields. Beans and squash seeds were planted between the hills of corn, and harvested crops were dried and stored for winter use.

Here we have a story of the constellation we know as the Great Bear. There are similar stories of the bear and its hunters among other tribes, especially the other Algonkian-speaking groups. This is a good example of the formalized opening, "they say that, a long time ago . . ." which makes it clear that the myth about to be told does not come from the teller's personal experience. And here, too, is an example of formalized ending, often used in telling great myths rather than in telling "little stories."

It is probable that this is only a fragment of a larger myth of origin and emergence, and that other parts of the original long myth have been lost.

▼▼▼▼▼▼

They say that once, a long time ago, it was early winter. It had snowed the night before, and the first snow still lay fresh on the ground. Three young men went out to hunt at first light, early in the morning. One of them took his little dog, named Hold Tight, with him.

They went along the river and up into the woods, and came to a place on the side of a hill where the shrubs and bushes grew low and thick. Here, winding among the bushes, the hunters found a trail, and they followed it. The path led them to a cave in the hillside. They had found a bear's den.

"Which of us shall go in and drive the bear out?" the hunters asked each other.

At last the oldest said, "I will go."

The oldest hunter crawled into the bear's den, and with his bow he poked the bear to drive him out. "He's coming! He's coming!" the man in the cave called to his companions.

The bear broke away from his tormentor, and out of the cave. The hunters followed him.

"Look!" the youngest hunter cried. "See how fast he's going! Away to the north, the place from whence comes the cold, that's where he's going!"

The hunter ran away to the north, to turn the bear and drive him back to the others.

"Look out!" shouted the middle hunter. "Here he comes! He's going to the east, to the place where midday comes from."

And he ran away to the east, to turn the bear and drive him back.

"I see him!" cried the oldest hunter. "He's going to the west, to the place where the sun falls down. Hurry, brothers! That's the way he's going."

He and his little dog ran as fast as they could to the west, to turn back the bear.

As the hunters ran after the bear, the oldest one looked down. "Oh," he shouted, "there is Grandmother Earth below us. He's leading us into the sky! Brothers, let us turn back before it is too late."

But it was already too late; the sky bear had led them too high. At last the hunters caught up with the bear and killed him. The men piled up maple and sumac branches, and on the pile of boughs they butchered the bear. That is why those trees turn blood-red in the fall.

Then the hunters stood up. All together they lifted the bear's head, and threw it away to the east. Now, in early morning, in the winter, a group of stars in the shape of the bear's head will appear low on the horizon in the east just before daybreak.

Next, the hunters threw the bear's backbone away to the north. At midnight, in the middle of winter, if you look north you will see the bear's backbone there, outlined in stars.

At any time of the year, if you look at the sky, you can see four bright stars in a square, and behind them three big bright stars and one tiny dim one. The square of stars is the bear, the three running behind him are the hunters, and the little one, that you can hardly see, is the little dog named Hold Tight.

Those eight stars move around and around the sky together all year long. They never go in to rest, like some of the other stars. Until the hunters catch up with the bear, they and the little dog can never rest.

That is the end of that story.

▼▼▼▼▼

Linguistic text recorded by William Jones, translated and revised by Truman Michelson. In: Boas, Franz, Handbook of American Indian Languages, Pt. 1, Bureau of American Ethnology, Bulletin 40. Washington, D.C.: Government Printing Office, 1911.

The Stars Above:
Long Sash and His People

No area of the United States has been subjected to as much anthro-
pological research as the Southwest. This is partly due to a pleasant
year-round climate, the contrast between desert bareness and the fer-
tility of valley farms, and the fact that a cosmopolitan non-Indian
society has grown up there.

But the wealth of anthropological research produced in the Southwest
is also partly due to the fact that here, as nowhere else in the United
States, has an aboriginal life continued, influenced but not completely
changed by the dominant culture that has surrounded it since Coro-
nado's invasion in 1540.

But, like all farmers everywhere, the village Indians of the Southwest
are keen weather-watchers, and their observations include sun, moon,
and stars. The sun and moon, like the earth, are deities. The stars are
supernaturals, and have less power over the lives of men than the
other heavenly bodies.

Pablita Velarde, of Santa Clara Pueblo, in her book Old Father, The
Story-Teller, *made these identifications of the stars mentioned in the*

59

*following story: Long Sash with Orion, the Endless Trail with the
Milky Way, the two bright stars at the Place of Decision with the
constellation of Gemini, the headdress at the Place of Doubt with
Cancer, and the three bright stars of helpfulness with Leo. However,
Tewa informants at Nambe and San Ildefonso Pueblos were unable or
unwilling to make any identifications for the present authors, even
with the aid of printed star maps. Hopi informants stated that they
knew the myth, but were unable to repeat it to non-Hopis, or to
identify the stars because of religious tabus.*

*Much of Pueblo mythology can be told only by certain persons under
certain conditions, because it is sacred in character. What stories have
been recorded in the southwestern villages are either the "little
stories," or fragments of the greater myths, parts which need not be
kept secret.*

*Storytelling in the villages is a winter occupation, and often the
storyteller constructs cat's cradles as an accompaniment to the tale.
This is the case with the star story told here. It leads directly into the
Tewa story of emergence and finding of a homeland, which is told in
the following section of this book. Actually, the two stories are parts
of a third, sacred myth, but since they can be told separately, they are
presented here in that way.*

▼▼▼▼▼▼

The bright star that rises in the east soon after autumn sunset is Long
Sash, who guided the ancestors of the Pueblos from the north to their
present home. He was a famous warrior, and the people followed him
because they knew he could lead them in defense against their enemies. Someone was always attacking the villages, and wrecking the
fields. The enemies captured women and children for slaves, and killed
many of the men, until Long Sash came to the rescue.

"Take us away from here," the people begged him. "Lead us to a
new land, where we can live peacefully."

"My children," Long Sash said, "are you sure you want to leave?
Life is hard here, I know, but it will not be easy anywhere. There will
be dangers on the way if you travel. Some will be sick; many will be
hungry and thirsty; perhaps some of you may die. Think, and be sure
you want to take that risk."

"We will face any hardships," the people promised him. "Only
lead us away from this dark country, to a place where we may have
light and life of our own."

So Long Sash started out, and the people followed him. They set their feet on the Endless Trail that stretches like a white band across the sky. This was the road they were going to follow until they found a place of their own.

As the people traveled along the Endless Trail with Long Sash, they began to grow tired and discouraged. Some of them quarreled with one another. They had little clothing and less food. Long Sash had to teach his followers how to hunt for food, and how to make clothing from feathers. At last he led them to a country that was so new that even Long Sash had never been there before.

In this new country there was no darkness, it was daylight all the time. The people walked and walked, and when they were too tired to go on they rested. Children were born and old people died and still they journeyed.

The quarrels grew more bitter, and the people began to fight among themselves, exchanging blows and inflicting wounds. At last Long Sash said to them, "This must stop. You are hurting yourselves worse than your enemies hurt you. If you are to come to the place of your own, there can never be violence among you. Now you must decide. We will stop here and rest. Many of the women are ready to have their babies. We will wait until the children are delivered and the mothers are strong. Then you must make your own decision, whether you will follow me or take another trail."

There where the two very bright stars are north of Long Sash in the sky, the people rested and made up their minds. Those two bright stars became known as the Place of Decision, and people look up to them for help today, when they come to the turning points in their lives. We all have decisions to make as long as we are on the earth: good or bad, forward or backward, kind or unkind. Those stars can tell us what to do.

When the people had rested and felt stronger, they were ready to go ahead with Long Sash. They told him so, and everybody went forward again. Long Sash watched, to be sure that his children traveled with good hearts and love toward each other.

But Long Sash himself was growing tired, and his own heart was empty and doubting. He heard strange voices speaking in his mind, and could not tell who spoke, or what they were trying to say to him. At last he decided to answer the voices. As he spoke to the unseens, his own people gathered around him to listen.

"Show me a sign to tell me who you are, fathers and mothers," Long Sash began. "My people are tired and I am growing old. Give me a word to tell me we are on the right path and will soon reach our home."

Then while his people watched him, frightened, Long Sash appeared to go to sleep. He dropped down where he had been sitting and his eyes were closed. He lay without moving while the people stayed beside him, because they did not know what to do. They grew more and more afraid.

At last Long Sash opened his eyes. He looked at the people who had gathered around him while he slept. "Don't be frightened," Long Sash told them. "I have been given many signs and promises. The worst part of your journey is over, and we will soon reach its end."

"That's good. Thank you," all the people said.

"Many people will reach this Place of Doubt in their lives," Long Sash went on. "When that happens, you should pray to the Above Persons, your fathers and mothers, for help and for guidance. In order to remind you of that, I will leave my headdress here, where people can look up and see it."

He laid his headdress down, and it became a bright, comforting cluster of stars.

And so the people went on traveling, and all the story of their journey is told in the stars above. Where there are three bright stars close together, they represent two young men who made a drag and fastened their load on it. Then, because there were two of them, they could add an old woman's load to the other two, and go on, pulling three loads on the drag. Those stars are a reminder of the helpfulness of the young men, and of their thoughtfulness of other people.

At last the people came to the end of their journey, and to the Middle Place which was to be their home forever.

▼▼▼▼▼

Told to Allice Marriott by Leonidas Romero de Vigil, Nambe, and by Maria Martinez and Antonio Da, San Ildefonso

Evening war dances at a powwow.

All photographs by Carol K. Rachlin unless otherwise noted.

Pots hung over open fire, cooking food for powwow.

Young dancer in full headdress.

An old Kiowa man at the Kiowa Gourd Clan powwow.

Quanah Parker (left) and friend after Peyote meeting. (*James Cox collection*)

Peyote ritual equipment (left to right): firestick for lighting cigarettes, water drum with drumstick, necklace of mescal bean and steel beads, gourd rattle with carved wood handles, and hawk-feather fan. The background is a Cheyenne ceremonial curtain.

Kiowa fan used in peyote ceremonies. The eagle-wing feathers are trimmed and notched for decoration, with "prayer path" carved on quills. Shafts are buckskin, topped by beaded handle. (*Dr. Harry L. Deupree collection, Oklahoma City*)

Part Two
THE WORLD AROUND US

How the People Came
to the Middle Place

The village, or Pueblo, Indians of the Southwest belong to several linguistic stocks but have a singularly homogeneous culture in all other respects.

Certain myths recur in all records of Tewa Pueblo life. One of the most generally distributed is that of emergence from the underworld into the light of day.

The Middle Place of this story's title might be taken as a characterization of Pueblo life as a whole. These Indians are the people of the middle way—of a life pattern in which one man does not seek to rise, economically or socially, above his neighbors; of a culture in which outward peace and harmony are sought as an expression of inward tranquillity and of rapport with the forces of nature.

Pueblo Indian life can be oversimplified or overelaborated in the descriptions written by non-Pueblos. In the sense in which the goal of life becomes an earthly Nirvana, Pueblo belief touches the dream-wishes of all men. In the high, clear air, the vivid coloring or sudden obliteration of all color under the scorching light of the Southwest, it is easy to believe such a state possible.

65

In the myth that follows, Spider Woman appears in her maternal characterization; the Twins are mischiefmakers, and their relationship to each other is less clearly defined than is the case in other myths of the same characters.

▼▼▼▼▼▼

In the beginning, the whole world was dark. The people lived underground, in the blackness. These people did not know that their world was dark all around them, because they had never seen the light. They had not been taught the difference between the black world underground and the blue sky world.

After a long time in darkness, the people began to get restless. Some of them said to one another, "Is this all the world there is? Will there never be another world?"

"There must be more of a world somewhere."

Then Mole came to visit them, digging his way along through the darkness with his little paws and sharp-pointed nails. The old men of the people asked Mole, "Is there more of a world than this, friend? You travel around, going far and fast underground. What have you found out? Is there more of a world somewhere?"

Mole answered, "It is true that I travel, and that I go far and fast in the darkness. Sometimes I go up, and sometimes I go down. When I go up, the world *feels* different. I think there is a new kind of air there, when I go up. I can not see the difference because I am blind and my eyes can not see the daylight as yours could. Maybe if some of you went up there and looked around, you could see whether there is another world above or whether all there is is here below."

"How should we travel?" the old men asked him then. "How shall we know where to go, or how to recognize that place when we reach it?"

"Follow along behind me," Mole replied. "I can tell you when we come out in that different world, because I will feel the change."

Then the people formed themselves into a line behind Mole, and he began to dig his way upward. He went up in a straight line and a slanting line and then a straight line again. As Mole clawed away the earth, the people took it from his little paw-hands and passed it back along their line, from one person to the next, to get it out of their way. That is why the tunnel that Mole dug upward for the people was closed behind them. That is why they could never find their way back to their old dark world.

When at last Mole stopped digging and the people came out in their new world, the light shone all around them and washed over them like a blessing. The people were blinded by the light, like Mole. Then the people became frightened. They hid their eyes with their hands, so that sight would not be burned out of their heads. Some of the people said, "This is as bad as the darkness. We can see nothing here, either."

Others said, "Let us go back. If we are to be blind anyhow, we will be safer in the world that we have always known. We can't see where we are in the darkness, but after all, we are used to that."

While all the people were standing there, arguing about what was best to be done, they heard a little small voice of a woman speak to them.

"Be patient, my children," the small voice said, "and I will help you."

The oldest man of the people asked her, "Who are you, my mother?"

Then she answered him, "Take your hands away from your eyes, but do it slowly, slowly. Now wait a minute. Move them a little bit farther away. Now, do it again. And again."

Four times in all the people moved their hands. At last their eyes were freed and opened, and the people could see her who had been talking to them. She was the bent little old Spider Woman, the grandmother of the Earth and of all living things.

Grandmother Spider sat on the ground before the people. Standing beside her were two young men, her twin grandsons, the War Twins. Grandmother said to the oldest men of the people:

"These twin grandsons of mine are silly. Now that you have come out in the Blue Sky World, I want you to act more wisely than they do. Look at them, the way they carry their weapons around with them. One has a bow and the other has a spear, and they both have throwing sticks. Those twin boys go around ready for war all the time. That is foolish, for people always to be fighting one another.

"I want you people always to remember this, and to stop whenever you are tempted to quarrel with one another. Never make yourselves weapons, because if you do you will be tempted to use them. And if you ever give in to that temptation, and do hurt to one another, then you will learn what sorrow is. To be happy, you must never hurt anyone in any way."

Then Grandmother Spider pointed with her lips and chin—away in the distance she pointed—and she said to the oldest man of all the people, "What do you see there, my child?"

And he answered her. "We see something green and growing, our Grandmother."

"That is right," said Grandmother Spider, "you see well. The name of that green growing thing is CORN, and it is food for all my people. You will have to learn to plant it and to care for it. You will have to weed it and hoe it and water it. You will have to work hard for the corn, but if you work right, with good hearts and love for each other within them, the corn will take care of you always.''

And the oldest men of the people asked her, ''Where shall we plant our corn fields, Grandmother?''

Grandmother Spider looked around her, and the people looked all around them, too. She asked them, ''What do you see, my grandchildren?''

And the old men of the people answered her, ''We see a red mountain in the east, Grandmother.''

Grandmother Spider told him, ''That is the Red Eastern Mountain [the Sangre de Cristo Range], and the snow on its slopes is stained red with the blood of the people who have died fighting the wild Indians who live on the east side of the mountains. Keep away from those mountains, my children, or the Comanches will kill you too. Now the daylight is going, and soon it will be night. Look again, quickly. What do you see over there?''

''There is a white mountain to the north, Grandmother.''

Spider Woman said to them, ''The name of that mountain is Mountain Standing [Taos Mountain]. If you go north of Mountain Standing, you will be cold, my grandchildren. The corn you plant beyond there will freeze in the ground, and it will never grow for you. So your home is not so far away, in that direction. Now, look again. What do you see over there, grandchildren?''

And the oldest man of all the old men of the people answered her, ''We see a black mountain in the west, Grandmother.''

Then Spider Woman said, ''That is Black Mountain West [Mount Taylor]. Behind it is the Place Where the Sun Lies Down and Dies. If you go too far in that direction, your corn will wilt and droop in the darkness, and will never grow and ripen. Keep away from the west, my children, or you will be back in the world of night.'' Then she said to them, ''Now, look again. What do you see in that direction?''

And they looked again, very quickly, almost glancing from the sides of their eyes, and the youngest one of all the old men of the people said, ''We see something golden and gleaming, far away to the south of us, Grandmother. It is too far away for us to be sure what it is. We can not see clearly enough.''

Then she answered, ''That is the Mountain of the South, the Turtle Mountain [Sandia Mountain], and when you reach it, you will know that you have reached your home.''

So the old men of the people asked her, "What means that word, turtle, our Grandmother?"

And in a voice that was growing tired and tiny, Grandmother Spider answered them, "When you find the signs of your two friends again—when you find Mole again and me again—then you will have found the turtle and his mountain that he carries on his back." And Grandmother Spider's voice faded as the daylight faded, and she and her twin grandsons were gone.

The people huddled together all that long night—the first night they had ever known, and the longest they would ever know—and waited for the daylight to return, half afraid and half hopeful that it would. They looked above them and saw the stars—hundreds and hundreds and hundreds of stars—white against the blackness like sparks that had scattered off the sun, and they watched as the stars walked across the sky. Some of the people noticed that certain stars were brighter than others, and they began to name them over to themselves, like naming new-born children.

When morning came, the stars faded and vanished. The people, standing there in full daylight, began to quarrel. Some wanted to go one way, some another. They all wanted to go straight to the mountains they could see most clearly, in the east, in spite of Grandmother Spider's warning. Those mountains looked closer to them than the Turtle Mountain she had told them was to be their home. They still couldn't see that mountain plainly. They couldn't quite make out its shape, or decide what a turtle looked like.

At last the people decided to travel to the Red Mountains of the East. There the Comanches surprised them, and before the people could defend themselves, many of them were killed. The white snow on the mountains was dyed red with their blood. Wherever you looked you saw still bodies lying. Wherever you listened you heard the last moans of the dying. That is why the mountains are called the Mountains of Blood—Los Sangres.

Now, today, in the east of the summer sky, you can see a feathered war bonnet. One Comanche man dropped it and forgot it and left it, on his way home, he was so loaded with the people's scalps.

Again the people quarreled among themselves, for some of them wanted to go south and others north. Some of these last people picked up sharp-pointed stones, like knives and spear heads, and hit their brothers with them. Then they ran away, to the north. When they came to the cold slope of Taos Mountain, a white bear came down its side, and breathed its cold breath on them. Some of those people fell down dead. Those who were left alive ran away, as fast as they could, sorrowing. The bear went back up the side of Taos Mountain, and on up into the sky. You can see him there in winter, early in the night.

Again the people began to quarrel among themselves about which way they should go. Some made themselves spears and spear throwers; they hurled the spears at their brothers and pierced them. And the men who were pierced fell down and died.

The others, weeping, ran away to the west, where the War Twins were standing. The twins shook their own weapons at the people, and threatened them, saying, "Go away, you foolish people, for this is the Place Where the Sun Lies Down and Dies. This is where every living thing must die. You can not stay here and live."

The frightened people ran away, while the young men stood and laughed at them. Then the young men turned their backs, and went back up the Black Mountain, into the sky. You can see them there in the springtime, about the middle of the night.

And again the frightened people quarreled, and some of them said, "At least let us go back to the place where we met our grandmother, the Spider. If she is still there, perhaps she can tell us what to do."

But the others said, "Where shall we find her? We have looked everywhere."

"We can go back to the place where we came out," said the old men of the people. The others were too tired to argue any more. They said, "Let us go back."

So the people turned sorrowfully away from the laughing War Twins in the western sky, and started traveling back. Their feet were tired; their sandals were worn out. They traveled back over the black lava beds (near Grants, New Mexico), and the knife-edged stones cut their feet. The people left a trail of bloody footprints behind them. You can see the red marks on the sharp black lava today.

But when the weary people came to the place where they came out, which was the Place of the Middle of the World, they could not find their grandmother again. When night came, they looked into the sky above their heads, and learned why they could not find her. For Grandmother Spider sat there in her star web, shaking her head and crying little star tears because her people were so foolish. Some of the people cried, too, and they ran away, up into the sky, to join their grandmother. The white road along which they ran is the Milky Way. On beyond it, in the summer, you can see the Spider's web. It is always there, so she can come back to her house whenever she wants to.

Now there were only two of all the people left, a man and a woman. They were very tired. Because there was nowhere else left for

them to go, they turned and journeyed south. Their road was hard.
They traveled through the desert, parallel to the course of the Rio
Grande, and it was dusty and sandy. At last the woman stopped and
looked around her.

"There are green trees over there to our right," she said.

The man looked at the dry world all around them, and he replied,
"Let us go over there and look at them. At least we can sit down in
the shade and be cool."

So they crossed the heavy sand of the Jornado del Muerto [Dead
Man's Road], and they came to the line of green trees. There was
another line, of blue water, shining beyond the trees. It was the Rio
Grande.

The woman said to her husband, "Indeed, this is a very beautiful
place. Let us sit down here and rest, for the world feels as if it would
be good to us."

After the man had rested a while, and felt stronger, he looked
around him. He said to the woman, "Look! There is a golden mountain over there, shining and gleaming, across the valley to the south. I
wonder what it is?"

The woman warned him, "Keep away from it. Stay away from it
forever. You know what happened to our people who went up into the
other mountains."

So the man sat still on the river bank beside her, but he sat facing
the golden mountain.

Presently the woman looked down at the sand beside her.

"Look!" she said to her husband. "Something is crawling along
the sand. I wonder what that little thing is, moving so slowly, slowly,
slowly?"

Then the man, in his turn, warned her. "Leave it alone. You know
what happened to the people who went near the dangerous animal, on
the Mountain of the North."

The woman obeyed her husband, and did not touch the little crawling thing, but still she watched it. Presently her husband began to
watch it, too, as it moved slowly along the sand before them.

The man said to his wife, "Look what a strange track this thing
leaves in the sand. We have seen tracks like that before, somewhere,
haven't we? They looked like the mole's tracks, don't they?"

The woman studied the little animal, and then she said to her
husband, "Look. Only look. Its back is as hard as a stone, but it has a
design carved and painted on it. Look! That design is Grandmother
Spider's web!"

Together the man and the woman watched the little crawling

thing. Together they said to each other, "Look! It is shaped like the Shining Golden Mountain!"

They looked again at the far away golden gleam of the mountain, which seemed to draw closer to them as they gazed. They looked down again at the little turtle, crawling along the sand. They looked at each other, and they smiled. They had found their friends Mole and Spider again, and their friend had shown the man and woman their home, as Grandmother Spider had promised he would.

You can read this, the end of the story, in the autumn stars. Look right directly above you for the man and woman, and the turtle who guided them home to the Middle Land, the land between the Rio Grande and the Sandia Mountain, the land that the Tewa Indians call their home.

▼▼▼▼▼

Told to Alice Marriott by Maria Martinez of San Ildefonso and Leonidas Vigil of Nambe Pueblo.

Nanih Waya:
The Sacred Bluff

CHOCTAW AND CHICKASAW

Originally, the Choctaws lived in what are now the states of Alabama and Mississippi. Among the southeastern Indians, the Choctaws were particularly noted as traders. They acted as middle men, often traveling long distances to barter the wares of one tribe with another. After the European invasion, the Choctaws replaced their dug-out canoes with pack horses. Soon paths along the banks of the Mississippi (Misha Sipokni) River and its eastern tributaries were marked by the hooves of little trotting Choctaw ponies laden with goods.

The story that follows contains several more or less familiar elements: the twin brothers, the recognition of a homeland and its identification with an actual location, and the tantalizing blend of myth and possible prehistory.

What is new in this story is the setting up of a pole to guide the people. The pole was an integral part of southeastern Indian ceremonialism. Whether in this case the leaning of the pole and its following have a Biblical derivation or not is impossible to determine. However, there are so many indications of prewhite life in the story that it is possible that the Bible story was not a source, but a support.

73

▼▼▼▼▼

Long, long ago, the ancestors of the Indians lived in a distant country, far away to the northwest. They hunted game in the forests, and built their towns on the river terraces where the floods could not reach them. For many generations the Indians lived in this land, and they were happy there.

But at last the time came when their fire was old, and they could no longer live in that place. They must find a new country somewhere.

The town chiefs called the people together for a general council. For four days they talked and debated, but they all knew the time had come to move, and that they must start their journey.

"Who shall lead us?" the young men asked. "We shall need strong leaders, if we are to find the new country."

"There should be one and there must be two," said the leading medicine man—a very old man, so old his ribs had fallen in. "We must be able to go forward, even if we should lose our leader."

"But what two are there who are equal to each other, neither one being first?" demanded the young men.

"Two who were born at a birth," said the old medicine man. "Let the twin brothers, Chatah and Chikasah, come forward and become our leaders, for they are brave and strong, and each is equal to the other."

Chatah and Chikasah stepped into the middle of the circle of councilors. "We are here, our father," they said to the old man.

"The people have called you," the old man told them. "You are the two who are one, who shall lead them to the new land. You must go forward bravely, for I will not be there to teach you. I will help you as much as I can, but I shall not go with you."

"How will you help us, our father?"

"Go into the forest and cut a young tree," the old medicine man directed. "Cut a sweet gum, and let it be tall and strong, but light and slender. Strip it of its bark and branches, and bring it here to me."

"We will do that," the brothers promised. Together they left the camp and went into the forest. They searched for a long time, and at last they found the tree they wanted: young and strong, tall and slender, light and easy to carry. The brothers cut down the sweet gum tree, stripped off its bark and branches with their stone knives, and carried it back to camp.

The old man was growing tired; he was so weak he lay on his mat in the thin late afternoon sunshine, so weak he could hardly speak. But when he saw the young men with the pole he seemed to gain in strength. "Lift me up," he said to the people around him, and when they had raised him till he sat, and had propped him with rolled-up mats, he called across the camp to the twin brothers.

"Bring the pole here to me," the old man directed them, and they laid the pole on the ground before him.

"Now bring me my paints," the old man said to his chief wife, and she brought the little buckskin bags of colors, and, as her husband instructed her, she mixed the paints with water in which sinew had been soaked. When she had filled two large shells with red and white paint, the old medicine man took them from her. Carefully he rose to his feet. Carefully he painted alternate red and white stripes around the pole, from top to bottom.

"Red is for war and white is for peace," the old medicine man said. "Remember, do not go to war if you can make peace, but if you must fight, fight till the blood runs red. Now lay me down."

The people laid the old man gently back on his mat and waited, but he was not ready to say good-by to them yet. "Set the pole up in the middle of the village," the medicine man directed. "Watch it, and see which way it leans. How does it go?"

"It leans to the east, our father," the twin brothers answered.

"Good, follow the pole," the old man said, and closed his eyes and died. The brothers covered his body with mats and raised a mound of earth above him.

The next morning, when the people awoke, the pole still leaned to the east. All the women packed their cooking pots in baskets, and the men took up their weapons. The twins lifted the pole. The children who were old enough walked, while mothers and fathers and older brothers and sisters carried the babies. And so the people set out, following the course of the river to the east, journeying to find their new home.

It was a long journey; the people traveled for many months and for many years. New lives came among them, for children were born along the way, and old lives were taken from them, for many of the travelers died. When that happened, the people did not leave the beloved bodies behind. They stripped the flesh from the bones, and buried it, but the bones they carried with them, for, said the people, "the bones are the heart of a man, and endure long after his flesh is gone."

After a very long time, the people came to a great river, the greatest they had ever seen. The people stood on the river's bank and marveled at it. "Surely this is where we should stop," said some of them.

"Let us wait here a while, at least," the women begged. "The clay here is good, and we can make new pottery vessels to carry our beloved bones in."

"We are tired," the children whimpered, and at last the brothers agreed to stay where they were for a little while. The women shaped the clay and fired the pots, and filled the vessels with the bones of their dead, and some of the men were selected to carry these precious burdens.

The sacred pole stood in the middle of the camp, all the time the people were working. Now, it leaned to the east and the south. It never straightened itself up and stood tall and erect, so the people always knew this was not the place that was to be their home, and that they must continue to search, farther and farther ahead.

When the people took up their burdens again, they followed the leaning of the pole to the southeast. First, with great trouble, they crossed the river. Until then the people knew nothing of boats. At first they tried to wade the stream, but it was too deep. Then they tried to swim it, but it was too wide. Some of the young and agile men crossed on tree rafts, but the women and older people were not able to do so. At last the twin brothers found a dry, sound tree trunk. With fire and their stone axes they cut away the wood, and hollowed out the first Choctaw dug-out canoe.

Then the people followed the stream, and because it was so great and wide they named it Misha Sipokni. In their language the name meant Beyond Age, for the river was so great that its source and its mouth were equally unknown to them.

And still they consulted the pole, morning and evening, and still it pointed to the south and east. Then one morning the pole pointed due east again, and the people left the great river Beyond Age and traveled again to the rising sun.

One morning when the brothers woke, they looked at the pole as they always did. It stood upright in the middle of the camp, so they knew they had come to the end of their journey. They looked around them. They were standing on the second terrace of a river, a good place to plant corn fields and build a village. But behind them rose a steep bluff, so there was not space for all the people.

"Now we must part," Chikasah said to his brother. "There is not enough land here to feed all the people."

"I am afraid we have to say good-by," Chatah agreed. Tears

rolled down his face and his heart was sorrowful. "Which one of us must go?"

"Let us ask the pole," suggested Chikasah, and the two brothers stood the sacred pole up between them. It fell toward Chikasah.

"Then I must go," Chikasah said, and he wept. "I must take my people and leave you. The pole is pointing north, and there I must go."

His brother answered, *"Fohah hupis hno yah,"* which means, "Rest all of us here." He looked long at Chikasah. "At least leave the beloved bones here with their friends," begged Chatah. "Let them be in one place with the friends they have known and loved."

"Where shall we leave them?" Chikasah asked, and Chatah replied, "Let us place them in this bluff; in this sacred mound of earth, as a symbol that we will always be brothers."

The people came together then, and worked to dig out the mound to make a burial place. When all the bones had been placed in the hill, the people wept together and mourned.

"Look at this great mound," they said. "It shelters our beloved elders and our friends. It is the symbol of our brotherhood, and every time the sun rises above it we are reminded that we are brothers. The place of the Fruitful Mound is our home forevermore."

That is how it came about that the sacred place of the Choctaws and the Chickasaws was at Nanih Waya, in Mississippi. That was the place where their last great council was held before they moved to the west again, under the pressure of the settlers and soldiers, to the Indian Territory west of the Mississippi—the river Beyond Age.

The first place where the Choctaws built a council house in their new western land was also called Nanih Waya, so that their hearts would always remember the place that they came from—the place that was their real and much-loved home.

▼▼▼▼▼

Compiled from fragments told to Alice Marriott by Choctaw and Chickasaw informants, and from Nunih Waiya, *by Anna Lewis.* Chronicles of Oklahoma, *Oklahoma Historical Society, Vol. 16, 1938, pp. 214–220.*

Additional material from: Wright, Muriel H., Guide to the Indian Tribes of Oklahoma. *Norman: University of Oklahoma Press, 1950.*

How the Half Boys Came to Be

In every North American Indian tribe there were objects of reverence, whose preservation was felt to be essential for the well-being of the people as a whole. There were also articles that possessed super- natural power to protect small groups, such as societies or individuals.

The Kiowas were protected by ten medicine bundles, known as the Ten Grandmothers. Guardianship of each bundle was handed from father to son and from mother to daughter, for each bundle had a male and a female guardian. Probably the first pairs of priests and priestesses were brothers and sisters, but as time went on and genera- tion succeeded generation, the guardians came to be unrelated to each other.

Each summer, during the Sun Dance, ten tipis were set up outside the main camp, and the priests and priestesses gathered in privacy to "clean" the medicine bundles ceremonially. This was done by prayer and song, and by fasting from sunrise to sundown during the period of cleansing. Sexual continence was observed by the participants and all members of their families during this period.

As part of the ceremony, the myth of the origin of the bundles was told; first the story of the Half Boys, and then, as each bundle was opened, the story of its contents. Only one priest knew each story, and since it could be told only within the closed circle, all the stories have never been recorded.

The Kiowas still reverence the Ten Grandmothers, and still make offerings to them, but the "cleaning" of the bundles, and the annual storytelling, have ceased. The ceremony probably has not been held since 1951.

▼▼▼▼▼▼

This is the holy story of the woman who went up to the World Above without dying. She went up while she was still alive and a beautiful young woman. There she met the Sun, and fell in love with him. He married her, and they had a child—a little boy.

All three lived in the World Above the World; the world that is behind the clouds, and so far away from human people and their problems that the human people never see it—just its flat blue floor which is the roof of our world.

But this wife was a human woman. There are many stories of how she met the Sun, but the one most people believe is that the Sun looked down one day and saw her swimming in the Washita River. She was so beautiful he sucked her right up out of the water, and took her home with him. And then, after about a year, their little boy was born.

The Sun went to his mother, and asked her, "Will you make my wife a tipi? She is a young woman, and she should have a tipi of her own." His mother agreed, and she made a beautiful white tipi for them, painted all over with the pictures of her son's war deeds. Above the stories of his battles she painted the design of his power. The young couple and their child lived very happily in the beautiful tipi.

Each morning when the Sun woke up he washed his face with last night's left-over clouds. While he was washing his face, his wife cooked breakfast, and when he had finished they sat down and ate their meal together. After breakfast the Sun took up his bow, and hung his quiver of arrows on his back. He was ready to go hunting, to get food for his family.

One morning, before he left to hunt, the Sun said to his wife, "What are you going to do today?"

"Oh, I think I'll go out and dig some roots," she replied. "It's a nice day, and the wild potatoes ought to be ripe. I think I'll take my digging stick and go and gather some. I've been hungry for wild potatoes."

"That would be good," the Sun agreed. "I'll try to get some deer meat to cook with them. Are you going to take our little boy with you?"

"Oh, yes," his wife told him. "I wouldn't want to go anywhere without my little boy."

"You can let him help you; he's big enough," the Sun said. "There's just one thing you ought to remember, and be sure you tell him about it, too. Both of you must never forget it. Don't dig up a wild potato if its top has been bitten off by a buffalo."

"Why?" his wife asked.

"Because it will bring you misfortune," the Sun answered. "That's all I know, so that's all I'm going to tell you."

He went away with his bow and arrows, and his wife took her digging stick. She and the little boy started out. When the child got tired from walking, his mother wrapped him in her deerskin robe and slung him between her shoulders. That was long, long ago before the Indians had horses. It was before they had to make big stiff cradles to carry the children safely when they traveled. All the mothers packed their babies on their backs in those old days.

The woman and the little boy wandered happily all day. She showed him how to use the digging stick, and by evening they had a skin sack full of wild potatoes. On their way home, the mother and child met the Sun coming along, coming back from the other side of the world, with a fat deer slung between his shoulders. That night the family had a fine dinner.

Next morning after breakfast, the Sun said, "Are you going out for wild potatoes again today?"

"Yes," his wife answered. "They're just ripe. Perhaps I can dig enough to dry some for the winter."

"That would be good," her husband observed. "But always remember, don't dig one if a buffalo has bitten off its top."

"I'll remember," his wife promised.

Sometimes during that day she wondered why her husband had made her promise not to dig a wild potato if a buffalo had bitten off its top. Not very often, but sometimes the thought would just cross her mind.

The woman went home that evening with such a big sack full of wild potatoes that her little boy had to help her drag it along. As the woman walked bent over, pulling at the sack, she noticed a wild potato plant beside the path, ahead of her. Its top had been bitten off. Maybe a buffalo did that, she thought. I'd better not dig it. Besides, I have enough to take home anyway.

The third day the mother and her little boy spent at home, drying wild potatoes. In the evening, the Sun said, "Don't you think we have enough potatoes to last us through the winter?"

"We have plenty," his wife answered, "but there are so many this year I think I'll make at least two more trips. Then if we have company we can give them dried wild potatoes to take home with them."

"All right," said the Sun, "just so you remember what I told you, and don't dig up the wrong kind."

So the wife went out a third time, and again she came home with such a big load of potatoes that it took her a full day to dry them all.

"Surely you have enough potatoes," said the Sun to his wife the next morning. "Even if we had a whole crowd of company, we would have enough presents to go around."

"Just one more day," his wife begged. "The season's short, and I don't want to run out of food."

"All right," her husband agreed. "Just so you don't forget what I told you."

The mother and son had gathered most of the wold potatoes that grew near their tipi. That day they had to walk a long way to fill their sack. Even after they had turned back to go home, the mother kept looking at the ground for the last few plants. She was almost home when she saw the same one she had noticed on the second day—the plant with its top bitten off by a buffalo. The woman stopped and she stood and she looked at the plant.

"I'll dig it," she said, half aloud, to herself. "It will just fill my sack, and I'm sure digging it up won't do any harm. That's just my husband's silly idea."

So the woman set her little boy down on the ground, and with her digging stick she pried the wild potato plant out of the ground. Instead of a groove in the earth where her digging stick had turned it, she saw that there was a hole, as large around as she was herself. Half afraid, the woman bent over and peered through the hole in the ground.

Below her, she saw the whole earth spread out. The prairies rippled with grass; the trees marked the river courses across the grasslands. She saw the great gray granite domes of the Wichita Mountains, and she saw a camp beside the hot springs that flowed from the north slope of Saddle Mountain. She could even see that the women in that camp were playing some sort of game.

They were her own people—her own Kiowa people. It could be

that camp she had walked out of to go swimming, the morning when the Sun found her and fell in love with her. The woman looked and looked. She strained her eyes with looking, but she saw no one in the camp whom she recognized.

For a long time the woman sat beside the hole in the sky, sometimes watching her people and sometimes crying with loneliness for them. The little boy grew tried and restless. He wanted to go home. He kept whining.

"Be quiet," his mother said finally. "Here, give me that last potato I dug up. Then we'll go home."

She replanted the last potato, and then they went home as quickly as they could, in order to get there before the Sun did.

After dinner that night, the woman told her husband, "I think you're right. We certainly have enough potatoes now to last all winter, even with company."

"Good," he said. "Then I'll start hunting buffalo instead of deer, and you and the boy can begin to dry the meat."

"Be sure you bring me home the tenderloins," his wife told him. "That's where the strong back sinew is, under the sweetest meat. I have to make winter moccasins for all of us, so I'll need a lot of sinew to sew with."

Every day, after that, the Sun went buffalo hunting. And every day, even if it was just for a little while, his wife slipped away to the hole in the sky, where she could peep through and watch her own human people. It was autumn in the world below, so the people there were hunting and drying meat, and the women were preparing sinew to stitch the winter moccasins.

Soon the Sun's wife had a great pile of sinew, so big that she hid most of it under her bed, where her husband wouldn't find it. She spent part of each day braiding a long, strong sinew rope. She would soak the sinew in water before she began to braid it, so the plaits of the braid were glued together. Her rope was as strong as any woman could have made it.

But still the woman asked her husband to bring home more tenderloin, so she could have more sinew to sew with. At first the Sun laughed at his wife for wanting to make so many winter moccasins. Then he noticed that the pile of dried sinew she kept beside the door of the tipi remained the same size even though he brought more sinew home day after every day. The Sun began to wonder about this, but did not ask his wife what she was doing. Instead, he watched her.

Whatever happened during the day, when the Sun came home at evening, his wife and child were safe in the tipi, cooking his dinner.

The Sun never once saw his wife do anything she shouldn't do. Like a good wife, she obeyed her husband in everything. And the Sun didn't think to look under her bed, so he didn't notice her sinew rope.

Each afternoon, when the wife had finished her work on the rope for that day, she left the tipi and went to the hole in the sky. Each afternoon she lowered her rope, and measured to see if it was long enough to reach the earth. And each day she had to return to her tipi and braid more sinew to lengthen her rope.

At last the afternoon came when the rope almost touched the ground. The woman was so happy that the tears of joy stood out in her eyes. She hunted all over, for a long time, and at last she found a mesquite root that was long enough and strong enough to hold her weight. She dug up the root, and set it in the earth beside the hole. Then she left the root in place, and went home to prepare her husband's dinner.

The Sun was the first to reach home that evening, and when his wife came in he asked her, "Where have you been? And what kept you out so late?"

"I've been gathering firewood," she answered, and indeed she had a bundle of wood on her back—all the mesquite sticks and roots she had found while she was looking for one that was strong enough to hold her weight.

The woman quickly built up her cooking fire, and began to cook the dinner. All the time she was cooking she was planning, for she was bound and determined to go home to her own people.

As soon as the Sun left to go hunting the next morning, his wife gathered up her rope and hurried to the hole in the sky. She tied one end of the rope to the mesquite root, and made sure that it was tight. Then she measured off half the length of the rope, and there she tied her son, fastening the rope securely around his waist. Whatever happens he will be all right, the mother thought, for he is a being who is made half-earth, half-sky.

Finally the woman tied the rope around her own waist. She stood beside the hole and lowered the half of the rope with the boy, so he hung midway between earth and sky. Then she began to climb down the rope herself. The loop of rope between the mesquite root and her waist swung down ahead of her.

The Sun's wife was in such a hurry to get home that she had forgotten that tying the rope around the little boy and herself would shorten it. When the woman reached the bottom of the rope, she still could not touch the earth. She and the little boy hung on the rope which swung in the wind. The tips of her moccasin toes barely brushed the tops of the grasses. The woman could not reach the earth, and she was too tired to climb back to the World Above the World.

The Sun came home early that evening, and looked for his wife and son. When he did not find either one, the Sun waited a while for his family to come in, thinking that perhaps they had gone farther looking for firewood than they planned. It had happened that way the day before. But still his wife and child did not return, and it was night. The Moon came out, and began to laugh at the Sun.

"Go and look for her," the Moon mocked him. "You who are so strong and powerful—go and look for your wife."

Even by moonlight, the woman's trail was easy for her husband to follow. She had been so excited and in such a hurry that she had left a plain, clear track.

Sun thought to himself, This trail is so clear, she must have come this way every time she went to gather potatoes. I wonder if she was silly enough to disobey me? I warned her. I told her plainly what she must not do.

He kept on following his wife's trail. You never can tell about women, the Sun thought to himself.

At last he came to the place where a wild potato with a bitten top lay on the ground beside the hole in the sky. Sun looked down through the hole and saw his son, hanging half way down, and the woman with her moccasin toes not quite touching the ground, just brushing the grasses as she swung back and forth.

Then the husband was truly angry. His son was frightened and crying, but he could not reach the boy to comfort him. It was all the mother's fault. She had wanted her own happiness too much to care about her husband and child.

Sun went back to the creek near his tipi, and found a willow tree. He cut off a branch and bent it to make a hoop. Sun bound the willow ring with a piece of fresh green rawhide, and the skin dried and hardened from the touch of his fingers. Then he laced rawhide back and forth across the ring, like a spider's web, and left a target hole in the center, so it was like the target ring for the spear-throwing game. It was the first Kiowa target-game ring that anybody ever made. When it was finished, the Sun painted the ring all over with red clay, for red was his own color.

Sun stood beside the hole, holding the ring in his hand.

"Go rolling down the sinew rope," he ordered. "Jump over the boy, and be sure you do not touch him. Keep rolling down the rope, clear to the bottom. When you reach the woman, hit her on the back of the head and kill her."

Sun spit on the target ring, to give it his power. Four times he spit on the target ring. Then Sun rolled the ring down the rope, and it went spinning along, jumping over the little boy, just as the Sun had told it to. When the ring got to the woman, she reached out for the grass, but her arms didn't stretch quite that far. If she could have touched the earth she would have been safe.

The ring hit the woman so hard it killed her. At the same time the mesquite root gave way in the World Above the World, and it fell through the hole in the sky. The woman dropped to earth. The little boy fell right on top of his mother, so hard that her belly split open.

When the boy waked from the shock of his fall, he didn't know what to do. He walked around and around. His mother was the only person he knew in this world, and she was dead. The boy was afraid to go too far away from his mother, so he stayed as close to her as he could.

Not very far away from that place where the woman fell to earth, a little old gray woman lived, all by herself. She had no one to hunt for her, but someone had given her one ear of corn, and she was wise enough not to eat it all. Instead, the old lady picked the grains off the ear, one at a time, and planted them in the ground in short little rows. Every day the old woman went from her tipi to her corn field, to work among the growing plants.

While the old lady was away her tipi stood open, because she didn't go very far from it. People who visited her could go into the tipi and sit and rest there while they waited for her to come home. The little boy, wandering away from his mother, found the old lady's tipi and went inside it. Suddenly he grew afraid. Suppose a horrible stranger lived in the tipi and came home and tried to eat him! Without looking behind him, the little boy ran away, back to his poor dead mother.

Then the old lady came home at nightfall. She looked around her tipi, and noticed the little footprints on the floor. "I wonder whose child it is?" she asked herself. "A little boy or a little girl? Oh, I'd be so happy if I could have a little child to love all day long."

But the poor frightened little boy had run back to his mother, who was the only one he knew in all the world, and though she was dead, he still tried to nurse at her breast.

The next day he was hungry, and more frightened than ever because his mother would not answer him or comfort him, so he went back to the tipi. But again he was frightened and ran away, and all the old lady found of him when she got home were the prints of his moccasins on the swept earth of the floor. She was delighted to see the footprints; she felt as if she would go crazy with joy because the child had come back. The old lady wondered and wondered how she could get the child, and keep it for her own.

The next day and the next day the old lady left food out where a child could reach it, when she went out to her corn field. When she came home the food was gone, and there were the moccasin prints all over her floor. The little boy was gone. He always ran away before the old lady got back.

The fifth morning the old lady made a girl's ball, of deer hair covered with buckskin. Then she made a dart game, with a laced rawhide target like the one that had killed the Sun's wife, and she made a small bow and some tiny arrows, and laid all the toys out on her bed, where the child would find them and could reach them.

When the little boy went into the tipi that morning, he found the toys and began to play. He put an arrow to the bowstring, and aimed it and shot it at the ball. The boy played with the dart game, too. But he didn't want anything to do with the ball except to use it as a target to shoot at. Balls were for girls to play with. The boy knew that, although no one had ever told him so. But still, late that afternoon, he ran back to his mother before the old lady got home.

When the old woman came in, she was overjoyed when she saw that the toys had been played with. "Oh!" she cried out. "It's a little boy! I'm so happy! I wanted a boy all the time! Now I wonder how I'm going to capture him?" And she thought and thought, until she had thought out a plan.

Early the next morning the old lady lay down on the floor of her tipi, as close to the wall as she could press. After a while she heard the little boy coming. He would come right up to the tipi door, and put his foot inside, and then draw back as if he were afraid. He did that three times. The fourth time he put his foot down, and stepped into the tipi. The old lady lay still and let him come all the way in.

The boy ran straight across to the bow and arrows, and began to play with them. When he was good and busy, the old lady stood up, in front of the door, and spoke to him. The little boy was frightened. He began to cry, and he struggled to get away from the old lady. But she held him tight so he didn't have a chance to get free.

Then the child began to beg. He said that he wanted to go to his mother. And the old lady told him, "You can't go to your mother; you haven't any mother. I will be your grandmother."

To comfort the boy, the old lady picked him up and put him on her back, the way his mother used to do. She sat down on the floor, holding him, and as soon as grandmother picked the little boy up his heart told hers all about his mother and everything that had happened to him. The old lady sat beside the fire, rocking back and forth to soothe the child, and singing to him:

> "Even though your mother has been dead a long time.
> You still are nursing at her breast,
> Poor thing, poor hungry thing."

She sang that song to her grandson, over and over. Presently the little boy quieted down as she held him, and went to sleep, cuddled against the old lady's back. He was hers.

The next morning the little boy asked the old lady, "What name shall I call you?"

She answered, "You can call me Grandmother, for I am the Spider Woman, the mother and comforter of all living things and beings."

And so the little boy called Spider Woman Grandmother, and she called him Talyi, or Little Boy.

They were very happy, living there in Grandmother Spider's tipi near the corn field. Grandmother made bowls of clay and baked them in the sun until they were dried and baked them again in her cooking fire until they were hard. She gathered the narrow-leafed yucca from the hills, and coiled and stitched it into baskets. Talyi helped her gather and dry wild plants to store for winter food, as he used to help his mother. Soon Talyi learned how to shoot small animals with his bow and arrows, and to clean his game and prepare the meat for Grandmother Spider to cook. She taught him everything a man is supposed to know.

Sometimes Talyi was naughty, or disobeyed, and Grandmother scolded him gently. Then one day she told him, "I have to go away today. I will be back before dark, but I want to take some of our fresh corn and dried meat to the Apaches to trade. We need salt."

"All right," Talyi agreed. "You can go on."

"Don't you want to go with me?" Grandmother asked.

"No," her grandson replied, "I'd rather stay here and play with my hoop and spear."

"You can do that," Grandmother agreed, "but be careful how you play. Don't throw your hoop up in the air, or something bad will happen to you. Mind me, now! Roll the hoop on the ground, and throw your spear through the target hole, but don't throw it up in the air."

"Yes, Grandmother," answered Talyi, but he wondered as he said this why Grandmother Spider told him what she did.

After Grandmother Spider had been gone for some time, and Talyi had eaten his lunch and taken a little nap, he began to think about what Grandmother Spider had said.

"Nothing bad will happen to *me*," said Talyi to himself, for after all he was his mother's son. "Everything will be all right. Grandmother is getting old, so she imagines things."

So he took his hoop and spear and went out of the tipi. At first Talyi rolled the hoop along the ground, but as he played, he grew more and more curious about Grandmother's final instructions. "Well, I guess I'll see what Grandmother meant when she said not to throw my hoop in the air," he decided, and he tossed the hoop as high as he could.

Up and up the hoop went, as high as the place where Talyi had hung down from the sky when his father's hoop rolled over him. Then, very slowly, the hoop began to fall. As it fell it came down faster and faster, until it struck Talyi on top of the head. The hoop went on down through Talyi's body, and cut him right in two. There was no longer one boy standing here, but two. They were identical in appearance, except that one was right-handed and one was left-handed.

"Well," said the right-handed twin to his brother, "here we are. Who are you?"

"I am I," the left-handed twin answered. "Who are you?"

"I am I, but when we are together we are we," his brother answered.

"Then *we* together must be stronger than either I," said the left-handed twin.

"Together we make one strong person," the right-handed twin agreed.

"Let us play with our hoop," the left-handed twin suggested, and his brother nodded.

So the boys played together, rolling the hoop along the ground and taking turns throwing the spear at it, until late in the afternoon. The shadows were growing so long that they melted into each other, and still the score was even. Then the boys looked through the dusk and they saw Grandmother Spider coming along, carrying the bundles of salt and mesquite meal she had traded from the Apaches.

"Oh, my," said the right-handed twin, "I wonder what she's going to say when she sees us? She'll be mad because we disobeyed her."

"I don't know what she'll say. I'm scared," said the left-handed brother.

Grandmother came closer and closer. She kept peering at the two boys, and shaking her head in bewilderment. "Talyi, where are you?" she called. "Who is that with you?"

"I am right here," the brothers answered together.

"Something is wrong with my eyes, for I see two of you," the old lady said, "and something is wrong with my ears, for you seem to me to speak with two voices."

"Nothing is wrong with your eyes or your ears, Grandmother," the brothers answered," for we are two who were one."

"Come close to me and let me look at you," Grandmother said. She passed her hands lightly over both boys. "You are two, two who were one," she admitted. "When there was only one of you I could keep him at home, to be company for me in my old age. But now that there are two of you, you have double strength. Now you must leave me and go out on your adventures, to save the Kiowas from the dangers that threaten them."

"Must we go now?" the twins asked her.

"No, my Half Boys," Grandmother reassured them. "You may wait until morning. But when the morning star shows in the east, you must go out. Find your enemies and destroy them, so the Kiowas may live long and well."

"Where will we find them?" the boys wanted to know.

"You will know who they are when you come to the place where they are," Grandmother answered. "Now let us feast together for the first time and the last time."

So in the morning the Half Boys went out to face their dangers and conquer their enemies. It is the trophies of those enemies that we know as the Ten Grandmothers.

Each time the boys were victorious Grandmother took the trophy and put it into a rawhide case, and honored it with her own name: Grandmother. There are ten sacred bundles, and each is called Grandmother by every living Kiowa. Grandmother Spider and her Half Boys will always remain in living memory.

▼▼▼▼▼

This version of the story was told to Alice Marriott by a Kiowa priest turned Christian, who has died since the telling. A similar myth is told in James Mooney's Calendar History of the Kiowa Indians, Bureau of American Ethnology Annual Report 17, pt. 2. *Washington, D.C.: Government Printing Office, 1892.*

Male and Female Created He Them: The River of Separation

*To many non-Indians, the Navaho are what their own name for them-
selves, Dené, implies—they are The People. Isolated in the desert
regions of the Southwest, the Navaho have survived drought and famine, the white man's diseases and his government's boarding schools,
to become the largest single ethnic unit of North American Indians
and a synonym for haughty independence.*

*The Navaho, along with other Athabascan-speaking groups from the
Northwest, generically known as Apaches, began seeping into the
Four Corners area where Arizona, Colorado, New Mexico, and Utah
join in the twelfth century A.D. At that time the Athabascans shared a
simple hunting culture, without pottery, basketry, or permanent
dwellings. In a century all that changed. The Athabascans raided the
settled agricultural Pueblo peoples, and learned agriculture, pottery,
basketry, and weaving from the captives they enslaved.*

*The Spanish introduction of sheep to the Southwest caused a flores-
cence in Navaho culture that still continues. With a permanent supply
of meat and of fibers for clothing assured, the Navaho came into their
own. Even their three years of captivity after the Civil War at the*

Bosque Redondo, near Fort Sumner, New Mexico, did not subdue the Navahos. Unlike the tribes of the Southeast, the Navaho resisted removal, and eventually, although decimated by hunger and disease, won by sheer stubborn resistance the right to return to their homeland near Canyon de Chelly, Arizona.

How much of Navaho mythology and religion came into the Southwest with the first migrants is a moot question. Certainly much of their ceremonialism was influenced by the village Indians with whom they came in contact. Yet the Navaho interpretation and performance of religion is their own; it has a robust quality that is foreign to Pueblo thought and behavior. Navaho religion is a religion of hunters, not of farmers, although the Navaho have practiced farming and sheep raising for centuries.

This myth has many northern elements. It is also told by the village Indians of New Mexico and the Hopi of northern Arizona, but its forthright character is distinctively Navaho.

The myth is included in this collection because it clearly illustrates the general North American Indian concept of duality, and of the need of two parts to become one. Like the preceding Kiowa story of the Half Boys, it demonstrates that the whole is greater than the sum of its parts.

▼▼▼▼▼

The people went through four worlds before they walked up a reed from the bottom of the Lake of Changing Waters into the present world, whose color is white. First Man and First Woman led the others, and with them came their two first children, the Changing Twins, who were half men and half women, and who could have no children ever.

On the surface of the earth, the people found a world unlike any they had seen before. There were mountains and plains, streams and trees, stones and growing plants. At first the people did not know how to live in this new world, but the Twins soon found out. One of them took some clay from the stream bed and held it in his hand, and it shaped itself into a food bowl. Then the clay he held formed a water jar, and again a dipper, and finally a pipe.

At the same time, the other Twin found reeds growing at his end of the stream, and with them he shaped a water basket, and a storage basket, and other kinds of mats and baskets. The Twins showed one another what they had made. ''These shall be the women's work,'' they said to one another.

''What shall the men's work be?'' the Twins asked each other. They looked around and saw stones lying on the ground. As the Twins picked up the stones, the pieces became axes and hammers, knives and spear points in their hands, and the men had weapons.

Last of all, the Twins shaped digging sticks from branches of mountain mahogany, and hoes from deer shoulder blades. Then the men had tools. They found the Kisani, a stranger people, living in the mountains and growing gardens in the valleys, and the people traded their tools and baskets and bowls and weapons for seeds to plant in their own places along the rivers. They learned how to build dams and spread the water on the dry ground where it was needed. The people were very happy, learning all their new skills.

Looking happily about them, the people saw four mountains standing at the Four Corners of the World, with a fifth mountain in their center. First Man, the chief of the people, named the mountain of the east the Dark Horizontal Mountain, and because people found pieces of white shell and white stones on its slopes, he gave it the color white.

In the south was the Great Mountain, where there were pieces of turquoise to be found, so First Man called it the blue mountain.

On Cloud Water Mountain, in the west, there was abalone shell, so it became the yellow mountain.

The northern mountain was the Home of the Big-Horned Sheep, for there were many of those animals on it. The color of this mountain was black, for both jet and cannel coal were to be found there.

The Mountain at the Center of the Earth was round and covered with many-colored jewels. On each mountain there was a pair of spirit guardians, male and female, and on each mountain there were birds the same color as the mountain. All the world went forward in beauty.

First Man and First Woman built their house near their corn field, and every day First Man went hunting while First Woman worked in her garden. They had a great many good things to eat, and they enjoyed eating. First Woman began to get fat, and as time went on and she ate the fine fat meats her husband brought home she grew bigger and bigger.

One evening, after they had eaten venison stew thickened with corn meal, and roasted pumpkin, First Woman leaned back happily against the wall. She belched loudly, and then she pulled up her skirt and patted herself between the legs, and said out loud, "Thank you, my womanhood."

First Man looked up, so startled that he didn't believe what he had heard. "Did you say something?" he asked his wife.

"Yes," First Woman answered, "I said, 'Thank you, my womanhood.'"

"That's not a nice thing to say," her husband protested. "That's a dirty way to talk."

"You don't always think it's dirty," First Woman sneered.

"Besides," First Man argued, "you know it isn't true. I'm the one who does the hunting and brings home the good food. It's me you ought to be thanking, not that old thing in between your legs."

"You wouldn't bring home all that good food if you didn't get something in return," his wife retorted. "That's why men go hunting—they have something to come home for."

"Oh!" shouted First Man, jumping up, "you think that's all a man cares about, do you?"

"Well, what else?" First Woman demanded.

"Lots of things," First Man said, stamping with rage.

"Name four," snapped his wife.

"I suppose you women think you could live without men," yelled First Man.

"I know we could," First Woman shot back. "I don't think the men could live without women, though."

They quarreled back and forth until they were both worn out, and then they lay down on opposite sides of the house. First Woman went right to sleep and snored away the rest of the night, but First Man lay awake, getting madder and madder, partly because of what his wife said and partly because this night she had turned her back on him. By daylight First Man was so angry that he got up and stormed out of the house.

"Come and listen to me, all you men," he shouted. "I want to see the men here, but the women can stay at home. I don't want to look at any women, the dirty things!"

"What has happened?" the other men asked as they came running up.

"Let me tell you what my wife said," First Man shouted, and he did.

All the other men were shocked, and their feelings were hurt, because First Woman had said such an awful thing.

"I'm not going to stand for it," First Man wound up. "I'm

going across the river and live on the other bank. Now it's a quiet
stream, but when the men and women live apart it will become the
River of Separation, and grow strong and fierce so that no one can
ever cross it.''

"We'll go with you," the men said. "If the women think they
can get along without us, let them try. They'll find out.''

So First Man waded into the river, and the other men followed
him. When they had crossed and stood on the opposite bank, a great
wall of water came down the river, like an arroyo in flood time, and
cut the men off from the women.

The men built shelters on the north bank for themselves, and the
women stayed in their old homes on the south bank. For a while
everything went well. Children were born in the women's village, and
when the baby was a boy his grandmother would go down to the bank
of the river and call out. Then one of the man-woman twins, who were
the only people who could cross the river, would paddle over on a raft
made of reeds, and take the boy baby back to his father. The girl
babies stayed with their mothers, and their fathers never saw them at
all. But within a year, of course, no more babies were born.

In the spring the women planted their gardens and corn fields
beside the river, singing love songs as they worked. Once in a while
one of the women would call across, "How are you getting along?''
and if the answer came, "All right. We're all fine,'' she would call
back, "Isn't there something you miss?'' And there was, but no
matter how much the men missed that thing their wives gave them,
they would not admit it.

The second year the women's gardens didn't do as well as they
had the first, and the harvest was smaller. The women began to get
thin and poor because they had no meat, while the men were growing
stronger and fatter—they had meat and gardens both. But no matter
how they starved, the women would not give in and cross the river.

At last a night came when First Man couldn't stand it any longer.
His food had no taste when he cooked it himself. He missed his wife's
good venison stews. He slept poorly alone in his blanket. The sun was
not as bright as it used to be, and he sat alone by his fire with water of
homesickness gathering in his eyes.

First Man got up and went out, and called the other men together.
"We have punished them enough, I think," he said. "We ought to go
back and take care of them.''

One of the other men nodded. "I can't stand to eat my own food
when I know my wife is hungry," he said.

"They must have learned their lesson by now," said a third man.

"We can forgive them now, I think," said the fourth. "They are starving with hunger, poor things."

First Man went down to the bank of the river and called across to First Woman, "Have you learned your lesson by now?"

First Woman, very tired and weak and thin, answered him, "We know we cannot live without our husbands."

"Will you say dirty things to me again?" First Man asked.

"Never! Never!" First Woman cried, weeping.

Then First Man called the man-woman Twins, and they came, bringing their raft, and ferried the men back across the river to their wives and their homes. The men bathed themselves, and dried their bodies with sacred corn meal, and then they went into their houses to their wives like bridegrooms.

From then on the River of Separation was a quiet stream again. When men and women crossed it, they crossed it together. For neither could get along without the other, and both had learned their lesson.

▼▼▼▼▼

Retold from: Matthews, Washington, Navajo Legends. *Memoirs of the American Folklore Society, V. Boston and New York, 1897.*

To Feed My People:
The Coming of Corn

▼▼▼ ZUÑI

Zuñi, in southwestern New Mexico, is the largest of all the Pueblos, and probably the most conservative, with the exception of the Hopi villages.

Zuñi was the first Indian community north of Mexico visited by Coronado in 1540. It was listed in the accounts of his expedition as the first of the Seven Cities of Cíbola, and was a great disappointment to the Spaniards. Instead of gold and jewels in lavish quantities, they found farmers and their families living in mud-walled houses.

At the time of the Spanish discovery, there were seven Zuñi towns, which today are consolidated into a single one, the Ant Hill at the Navel of the World, near Gallup, New Mexico.

Zuñi religion and philosophy are extremely complicated, and have furnished lifetimes of study for some of the greatest of American anthropologists. What is told here is only a fragment of the immensely detailed origin myth.

The origin myth is recited annually, by two priests speaking in uni-

96

*son, in midwinter. Then the Shalako, great birdlike supernatural
beings, also known as the Divine Ones, come to bless the houses of
Zuñi in a night-long ceremony of song and dance. The recital of the
entire myth occupies two to four hours early in the performance, and
if a single syllable is missed or slurred the dance will not result in
health and well-being for all the people.*

*The Zuñi language is unrelated to any other, and Zuñi music is
unique in North America, for it provides for two- and four-part harmony.*

▼▼▼▼▼▼

The first people who came into this world were the Áshiwi, and they
were very queer-looking. They had short tails, with no hair on them,
and very long ears. When the Áshiwi lay down at night to go to sleep,
they lay on one ear and covered themselves with the other. Their
hands and feet were webbed, and their heads and bodies were covered
with moss, with a big tuft of it sticking out in front of their foreheads
like a horn.

All the same, the Áshiwi were human people, who moved about the
earth, looking for the place that was to be their home. At last they
found a place they liked, beside a spring, and agreed that they would
settle there. Then the Divine Ones visited the Áshiwi and cut off their
tails and shortened their ears. They told the people to bathe in the
spring and become clean, and when the Áshiwi came out of the water
all the moss had been washed away from their bodies and heads, and
they looked like any other human beings.

After the Áshiwi came out into this world, other people followed
them. First came the Hopis, who had been neighbors and friends of
the Áshiwi in the underworld. Then came the Mexicans, and then the
Coconino and the Pima, and finally the Navahos and the other
Apaches. Now the world was populated indeed. The Áshiwi found the
middle place of the whole world, and there they established Zuñi,
where it is today.

Now on the way up from the underworld, some of the Áshiwi had
become tired and had fallen behind the others. Once there was a
settled place for them to come to, these people began coming out,
sometimes a few at a time, sometimes many at once. Each time some
Áshiwi joined the others, the earth would rumble and tremble, as a
sign that the people were coming out. Then the people above would
say, "Here comes my younger brother," or, "Look, my little sister is

coming out." And they all rejoiced, and were happy to be together again.

This went on for a long time. It would be too hard to say how long it took in years, but four magic cycles were completed before the last of the people emerged from the underworld.

The last to come out were two witches, a man and a woman. In their hands the witches held all power, for good or for evil. The Divine Ones heard the rumbling before the witches emerged and came to meet them. The supernatural beings were surprised to see two people with their heads covered with hoods of coarse fibers, which blew loosely about their shoulders in the breeze.

"Where are you going?" the Divine Ones asked. "We don't know whose relatives you are."

"We would like to join your people at the Middle Place of the World," answered the witches.

"We don't want you with us," the Divine Ones said.

"Oh, but you will," the witches answered. "See how we hold our hands, clutched under our armpits? In our hands we grasp all the seeds of the world. If you do not let us go to the People of the Middle Place we can destroy the world, for we hold all the seeds, and without them men will starve."

"Perhaps the People of the Middle Place will not want you," the Divine Ones insisted.

"We have all sorts of precious things here," the witch went on as if he had not been interrupted. "I will give these seeds to the leader of the village, but in return he must give us two of his children, a boy and a girl. When he gives us the children, the corn and other seeds will belong to him."

"Why must he give you his children?"

"So that they may die. If they do not die, the rains will never come and the seeds will never grow."

"Wait here," directed the Divine Ones, and they hurried away to the Middle Place. They came to the head man of the village, and told him what the witches had said.

"Will they really hold back the rain if I don't give them my children?" the head man cried.

"So they said," replied the Divine Ones.

"Then it is well," he assented, and he bowed his head.

When the witches reached the Middle Place they went to the head man. "We have come for your children," the witches told him.

"I have no small children," the head man informed them. "I have only a youth and a maiden, but you may have them if you wish.

What do you want to do with them?'' For he still hoped that his children might be spared.

"We wish to destroy those young people," said the witches.

"Must you? Must you really destroy my children? Why do you say that?"

"If we don't destroy them the rain will never come," answered the witches. "It is only by destroying those children that rain can come for all the people. We have wonderful things to give you, but there must be much rain if those things are to be of value to you."

"It is well," the head man repeated, and he led the witches to his house, where his son and daughter were sleeping in an inside room.

The witches touched each child over the heart, and shot their magic power into the young bodies, so the children died.

"Now bury them in the earth," the witches instructed the head man, and he did as he was told.

Four days and four nights the male rains fell, heavy and strong, soaking the earth and making it ready to bring life to the seeds. Then on the fifth morning the earth began to rumble. The Divine Ones, watching, saw the young man rise from his grave, alive and well.

Again the rains, the female rains, fell, soaking the earth, gently stroking it so it would bring life into the seeds. On the fifth morning the earth rumbled again, and the girl stepped out of her grave, unharmed.

That night the witches planted their seeds, and by morning the corn stood in rows above the earth. "Come and see," the witches called to the Áshiwi, and everyone came and stood beside the field, watching the corn grow through the day. By evening the corn was ripe and ready for harvest, and the witches called to the Áshiwi again. "Come and eat," they said.

The Áshiwi tasted the food, but it was hot, like chili pepper, and they did not like it. "It isn't fit to eat," they said to the witches.

So one at a time the witches called the crow, the owl, and the coyote, and those three tasted the crops. As the birds and the coyote ate, the food became milder and mellower, so that at last it was just right. The Áshiwi ate the crops, and liked the food.

But from that time forth the people had to watch their fields, for the crow and the owl and the coyote like the food so much that they will steal it all from the farmers if they can.

▼▼▼▼▼▼

Told to Alice Marriott by informants who prefer their names withheld.

To Feed My People:
The Coming of Corn

So far in this book, we have dealt with the great myths of emergence and creation, and there are more stories of a serious character to come.

The one that immediately follows, however, is one of the "little stories" told for the instruction of children by Cheyenne grandmothers and grandfathers.

In winter, in the evenings, it was customary to send through the village for an older man or woman who was known as a good storyteller. As the village crier made his rounds, children and adults followed him, to gather in the host tipi where a feast, often of dried fruit or of intestines stuffed with pounded meat—like sausages—and roasted over the fire, had been prepared.

The storyteller sat in the place of honor on the west side of the tipi, and the other people lined the curve of the tipi walls, with the children nearest to him.

Once the story was begun, everyone in the tipi must stay awake. If a child went to sleep, the storyteller could simply stop talking and go

home. There was a standard beginning and ending for each story.
According to Cheyenne belief, if the little stories were told in summer,
storyteller and listeners alike would "grow a big humpback."

That the story of corn became instructional rather than sacred is
probably the result of the Cheyenne transition from horticulture to
hunting. During the historic period, the sacred stories of the Chey-
enne have dealt with buffalo and other animals.

▼▼▼▼▼▼

Once, a long, long time ago, men would go away from the main camp
to hunt. If they expected to be gone a long time, they took their
families with them. Then they camped away from the main band until
the hunt was over.

One man took his wife and his little boy on a hunting trip close by
Rosebud Creek, in Montana. The Cheyennes called it Tomato Creek in
those days, because wild tomatoes grew very thickly there. So they call
this the Tomato Creek story.

It happened late in the fall. The father went out to hunt, but he
must have got lost or killed or something, because he never came back.
So the mother and the little boy waited and waited for him. They
didn't have anything to eat at all. All they had in the world was the
tipi they lived in.

Every day the mother went out looking for food, but all she could
find were wild rose hips. Wild tomatoes was what the Cheyennes
called them then. The mother brought the rose hips home, a few at a
time, and she and the little boy made soup from them. It was all they
had to live on.

One day, when the mother had gone out gathering, somebody
opened the tipi door. He peeked in and looked all around.

"Are you all by yourself, little boy?" he asked.

"Yes," the little boy answered.

"Can I come in and play with you?" questioned the stranger.

"Yes, if you want to. Come on in," said the little boy who lived in
the tipi.

When the door opened and the stranger stepped through, he was
another little boy, about the same age as the one who lived in the tipi.
But the little boy who lived there was all thin and pitiful, while the
new little boy was as fat as he could be, with big round cheeks and
eyes and stomach.

So the strange little boy stayed and the two children played inside the tipi, because it was too cold to go outside. After a while, the stranger stood up. "I'm ready to go now," he said, "but before I go I want to make you feel good." Then he danced, and he sang:

> "Little child is alone,
> Little child is alone.
> They might eat me!
> They might eat me!
> Heyeheh!"

And then he ran out of the tipi.

Late that evening the mother came home with her little handful of wild tomatoes. She had walked all day, to find so few! "What are you excited about, son?" she asked.

"Oh, Mother, I had company today! We had the best time! We played together all day!"

"Who was your company?" the mother wanted to know.

"I don't know his name," said the little boy, "but he's about my age, and he's a nice boy. And he sure is fat—as fat as he can be—all over. He wants to come back tomorrow and play some more. I told him he could."

"All right," said the mother. "I'm glad you have someone to play with, when I have to be away so much."

Before the mother went out the next morning, she said to her little boy, "I don't understand about your playmate, but it's all right for him to come and play with you. Try to find out something about him, if you can."

Soon after the mother left, the tipi flap was lifted, and the fat little boy peered in. "Where's your mother?" he asked.

"She went out to gather wild tomatoes," the thin little boy said. "That's all we have to eat. She has to walk a long way and look hard at all the bushes before she finds them."

"Then I can come in," said the fat little boy, and he jumped into the tipi.

The two children played happily all day, and when the dark was coming the fat little boy danced and sang again:

> "Little child is alone,
> Little child is alone.
> They might eat me!
> They might eat me!
> Heyeheh!"

And again he ran out of the tipi.

And the third day the same thing happened.

That evening, after they had eaten their poor soup and were sitting beside the fire of little sticks that was all they had to keep the tipi warm, the mother said to her son, "I've been thinking about your friend and his song. I can't get it out of my head, that part about, 'They might eat me, They might eat me.' "

"What do you think it means, Mother?" her little boy asked.

"I don't know," the mother replied, "but I'm going to find out."

She took her knife from its sheath at her belt, and whetted it against a flat stone until it was as sharp as sharp.

"Now," the mother said, "tomorrow morning take this knife, and hide it under the bend of your knee as you sit beside the fire. Sit as still as you can all day, so the knife will be hidden. Then when the fat little boy begins to dance and sing, you put the knife right through his stomach."

"All right," said her son. He felt sorry for his playmate, but still he knew that his mother would not tell him to do something that was wrong.

So the next day the fat little boy came again, but this time he seemed to be nervous and frightened, as if he were not sure what was going to happen. He put his foot through the tipi door three times before he finally entered. Then he said, "Why are you sitting there by the fire? Come on, get up! Jump and play the way we always do!"

"I'm too tired," said the little boy who lived in the tipi. "I don't get enough to eat. If I were big and fat like you, I could jump around and play all day. But I'm poor and skinny, and I get too tired to play."

"Well, you can sit and watch me, then," said the fat little boy, and he began to dance and play around the tipi. Early in the afternoon he stopped playing, and said, "This isn't any fun, playing all by myself. I think I'll go home."

But before Fatty left, he stood in front of the poor thin little boy and danced and sang one last time. When the fat one got to the part of the song about, "They might eat me," the other little boy reached over and jabbed his knife right in the middle of the fat one's stomach.

Grains of corn began streaming out of him like blood, and the fat one turned and ran away as fast as he could go. The corn fell to the ground behind him, to mark his trail.

The poor little boy ran out of the tipi. "Mother! Mother!" he called.

The mother was hidden in the brush by the creek, and when she heard her little boy calling she ran out to him. "What is it, my son?" she asked.

"Look!" said the little boy, pointing to the corn on the ground. "I don't know what it is, Mother, but it ran out of him. What is it? Did you ever see it before? Maybe it's good to eat."

"I don't know what it is. I never saw it before," the mother answered, but she picked up a grain of the corn and tasted it. "It's sweet and good," she said to the little boy. "You can taste it too."

Then the two of them followed the trail of the corn down and along the creek. At last they came to a buffalo calf skin lying on the ground, filled with more corn.

Then the mother raised her arms, and gave thanks to Maheo for the blessing he had sent them. They gathered up the sack of corn, and, as they went back to the tipi, they picked up every grain of corn that had dropped along the path, and saved it.

The mother and the little boy had all they could eat for the rest of the winter. In the spring, the band came back and found the mother and child. The hunters divided their meat, and the woman divided her grain, so from then on all the Cheyennes lived well.

Let the next teller tie a tail to that story.

▼▼▼▼▼▼

Told to Alice Marriott by Mary Little Bear Inkanish.

To Feed My People:
The Coming of Corn

▼▼▼▼▼▼▼▼▼▼▼▼▼▼▼▼▼▼▼▼▼▼▼▼▼▼▼▼▼▼▼▼ MIKASUKI

*The Mikasuki are one of the two groups of Indians who live in Florida
and are known collectively as Seminoles.*

*The Seminoles generally are attractive people—good to look at, proud,
independent, and withdrawn from strangers whose bona fides have not
been tested. In Seminole camps can certainly be found the last rem-
nants of the native culture of the southeastern states, and probably of
the circum-Caribbean area.*

*Today a large part of Seminole economy is based on tourism. There
are "camps" along the Tamiami Trail and on the outskirts of Miami
and its suburbs. Here the Indians live in native thatched huts, or
chickees, work at crafts for sale to tourists, and indulge in exhibition
wrestling with alligators. Periodically attempts are made to "im-
prove" the Seminoles' lot and to prevent their "exploitation." Frequently investigations disclose that the Seminoles are "exploiting"
themselves and the tourists, and that an important part of family
incomes is derived from a way of life which the Seminoles find as
fascinating as their visitors do.*

105

*Deep in the Everglades, however, Seminole villages, with their scat-
tered corn fields and gardens, still cluster near ceremonial dance
grounds. Planting and harvest ceremonies are held. Native crafts flour-
ish. Children are sent to school, but when they are at home they
receive instruction in Seminole traditions and history.*

*The story that follows has a surprisingly wide distribution in North
America. It has been recorded from the Mikasuki, the Creek-speaking
northern Seminoles, the Iroquoian Cherokee and Seneca, and, of all
unlikely places, from the Keresan-speaking Pueblos of the Rio
Grande. If any one myth can be said to represent the original corpus
of North American mythology, this is probably the one.*

*The death-and-resurrection theme is recurrent in every version
found—indeed, in every corn origin myth known. Only through the
death of the parent seed can the living plant come into being. Whether
the theme be stressed or not, it is omnipresent, as it is in the mythologies of agricultural peoples the world over.*

▼▼▼▼▼

Two brothers lived with their grandmother in a chickee in the Big
Cypress Swamp. The old lady kept the house and did the cooking, and
the two grandsons went out hunting every day. They were fine hunters. They brought in birds and rabbits, fish and eels; they brought in
big game, too—deer and wild turkeys.

They lived in a fine chickee. The uprights were made of cypress
poles, and the roof was thatched with palmetto. Every spring the
young men gathered fresh palmetto fans, and the old lady braided
them into the old ones to make the roof thicker and tighter. The floor
of the chickee was raised as high above the ground as a flea can jump,
and the rafters were set close together so there was plenty of room
above them to store whatever the family had. Off to one side was
another storehouse, for dried food, and the old lady had her grandsons
build that with solid paling walls so no one could see into it.

One morning the old lady looked out of the door, and saw her
grandsons sitting in the dooryard, cleaning their guns. The hibiscus
were in bloom, and in the deep heart of every other blossom sat a little
frog, greener than any leaves. The hummingbirds were lighting up the
trumpet flowers like sparks dancing above a fire. It was a beautiful
morning, but the twin grandsons sat there, cleaning their guns, and
looking as if they didn't have a friend in the world.

"What's the matter with you boys?" their grandmother asked

them. "It's a beautiful morning, and all the world's alive and singing. Why do you look so sorry?"

"We're tired of always eating meat," Older Brother said. "Why can't we have something else to go with it, for a change?"

"Meat is God's food that he has given you," the old lady replied.

"God is great," said Younger Brother. "If he can give us all the different kinds of meat, perhaps he can give us other foods, too. Then we won't kill so many of His animals, and we won't get so tired of eating them."

"That's an idea," said the grandmother. She stood and watched the boys while they finished cleaning their guns, and then she asked, "What kind of meat do you plan to kill today?"

"Deer," said Older Brother.

"When you come home with the meat, part of the dinner will already be cooked," Grandmother promised. "It will be the most delicious food you ever ate, and we will cook the deer meat to go with it."

All day, while they hunted, the brothers thought and wondered about what their grandmother had told them.

"Do you think she can do it?" Younger Brother asked.

"She's very strong," Older Brother reminded him. "She has a lot of power. I believe maybe she can."

Late in the evening, when the first mists were rising from the bayous, and one little star was trying to show itself off in the west, the brothers came home. As they came near the chickee, they smelled a food-smell that was like perfume.

"Grandmother! Grandmother!" Older Brother called out. "What are you cooking that smells so good?"

"Clean and butcher your deer, and when the meat is cut up, bring it to me," Grandmother instructed them. "Then you will soon taste the most delicious food in the world."

So the boys hurried with their butchering, and when they had the meat cut fine and small, they took it into the house and gave it to their grandmother.

"Thank you! Thank you!" Grandmother said. She lifted the lid of her cooking pot and dropped in the meat, and the smell of the food was so good the boys' mouths watered.

It was a young deer and the meat was tender, so it was quickly cooked. Then Grandmother put the wooden bowls of food on the platform of the chickee, with a wooden spoon for each one, and called to her grandsons, "Come and eat."

The food in the bowls tasted like nothing the boys had ever known before. It was sweet and delicate; it melted on their tongues. "What is it, Grandmother?" they asked her.

"It is called corn," the grandmother answered, and that was all that she would tell them about it that night. When the boys had eaten all that they could hold of the wonderful corn, they went to bed and slept deeply.

In the morning, the grandmother again looked out, and again she saw the boys cleaning their guns. This time their faces were broad with smiles, and they looked as if they loved the whole world.

"What are you going to hunt today?" Grandmother asked.

"Wild turkeys," Older Brother replied. "We thought they would taste good if they were cooked with corn."

"Wild turkeys are always good," his grandmother agreed. "To-night, though, I will have another new food for you, in case you get tired of eating corn."

"What do you think that new food will be?" Younger Brother asked, as the two boys entered the woods.

"I don't know," Older Brother replied, "but I don't think I will like it as well as corn, whatever it is."

But all the same the boys were in such a hurry to taste their new surprise dinner that they drew and plucked the wild turkeys they had shot as they walked along the path on their way home. When they got to the chickee, the twins smelled the new food cooking. It smelled like corn, but at the same time it smelled different, with a perfume of its own.

"I see that I won't have to wait long for you to cut up the meat," was all their grandmother said. She took the wild turkeys over to the cooking fire and plopped them into the pot, and soon the meal smelled better than ever.

"Come and eat," Grandmother called to the twins, and when they had washed their hands and faces at the water jar, they came in under the thatched roof, filled their bowls from the cooking pot, and began to eat.

"What is this food called?" Older Brother asked his grand-mother, when he and Younger Brother had eaten all that they could hold.

"It is called grits," Grandmother said. "It is another of the gifts of corn."

The next day the boys killed muskrats, and as they came near their home a new delicious smell met them.

"Where does Grandmother get all these foods?" Younger Brother asked of Older Brother.

"I don't know," Older Brother answered, "but maybe we can find out. Tomorrow, when I go hunting, you hide in the clump of trees behind the house. Watch and see what Grandmother does. Then perhaps we will know where these corn foods come from."

That night Grandmother had a pot of dried cracked corn simmering on the fire. She cut the muskrats into it, and when the meat had cooked the brothers ate their fill.

"Oh, that was good, Grandmother," they told her. "That was delicious. How many ways are there to cook this corn food?"

"No one person will ever know how many," Grandmother answered. "No one person can ever live long enough to take all the good gifts that corn has for mankind."

The next morning the brothers left home together, but when they reached a wild orange grove a little away from their home the Younger Brother dropped back and hid, and Older Brother went on alone.

It seemed to Younger Brother that he waited a long, long time, hidden in that orange grove. It was mid-June and the trees were loaded with blossoms. They were as perfumed as cooking corn, and Younger Brother grew hungry, waiting there.

At last he saw his grandmother come out from the chickee, and go to the storehouse. The sun was high in the sky, so Younger Brother knew that it must be midday, the time when Grandmother usually started to cook their evening meal. He slipped through the grove without a sound, and at length he reached a place where he could peek through the open door into the darkness of the storehouse.

Younger Brother saw Grandmother spread a dried deer skin on the floor, and place a wooden bowl beside it. Then she stood on the hide, and rubbed her open palms down her sides. Wherever Grandmother's hands passed, grits tumbled from her body onto the deer skin. When she had enough grits for their evening meal, Grandmother gathered the edges of the deer skin together, and went back to the chickee.

Younger Brother turned away, and walked quickly along the hunters' path to meet Older Brother. When they came face to face, Older Brother asked, "Did you find out where our grandmother gets the corn?"

"Yes," Younger Brother replied, "it is part of herself. She rubs her hands against her sides, and the corn falls on the earth for her to gather up."

"That's impossible!" Older Brother exclaimed. "Why would she want to do that? Why does she think we want to eat our own grandmother? Only Caddos and Tonkawas are cannibals! Mikasukis would never eat anybody.''

They hurried home, and dinner was waiting for them. Grandmother had added dried turkeys from the storehouse to the grits. Even though the food looked tempting and smelled delicious, the brothers could hardly swallow it.

"What's the matter?" Grandmother asked them. "Aren't you hungry? Don't you like my cooking, all of a sudden?"

"The food's as good as always," Older Brother said. "We're just too tired from hunting to eat much, that's all."

"Aieee!" Grandmother cried, and she fell to the floor, almost without life. The brothers picked her up and laid her on her pallet in the chickee.

"What can we do to help you?" Younger Brother cried. "Dear Grandmother, what has happened? What is it you have felt, to make you so sick?"

"You have found out my secret," Grandmother barely breathed, without opening her eyes. "Now that my secret is known, I must prepare to leave you soon."

"Dear Grandmother, don't die!" Older Brother begged. "Stay with us; don't leave us. How can we live without you?"

"I will always be with you," Grandmother assured him, and slowly her eyelids raised, and her eyes lay open in her gray face. "When I am gone, you must do exactly what I am going to tell you. Bury me in the field near the bayou; the field that never floods. Lay my body in the earth, and cover me with the rich soil. Then build a fence of sticks all around my grave, to keep out the wild hogs, and don't let anyone come near my burial place. Next spring, you will see something green come out of the earth where I am buried. The plant will grow tall, tall. Its top will blossom. There will be beautiful tassels along its sides. Leave my plant alone, and in the fall, harvest the heads that bear the tassels. Dry the grains, and store them in a clean dry place where the rats can not get them, until next spring."

"What shall we do then, Grandmother?"

"When the corn is dried and laid away, go out into the world, and find yourselves wives. Bring them home, and when spring comes let them plant the corn. Make little hills in rows in the fields, and plant four grains of corn and four beans in each hill. Then the corn and beans will grow together, and you may plant their little sister, the squash, between the rows. If your wives take good care of their gardens, then you will always live well, because you are both good hunters. As long as you have the corn, I will be with you."

Then Grandmother sighed, because she was old and tired and she had given up all her power. Before she died, she blessed her grandsons, and wished them well with their lives, their wives, and their gardens.

And the grandsons obeyed the old lady, and buried her as she had instructed them to. Then, in the fall, when the corn was harvested and dried and stored, the two brothers went out and found wives for themselves.

So corn came to the Mikasukis, and so the Mikasukis learned to garden.

▼▼▼▼▼

Told to Alice Marriott by Seminole informants.

To Feed My People:
The Coming of Buffalo

Of all the southern Athabascans, the Jicarilla Apaches are, even today, probably most feared by their neighbors. Their reservation in north central New Mexico is a high plateau, surrounded by heavily wooded mountains, and from this fastness they were accustomed, from the beginning of the thirteenth century, to raid the Rio Grande Pueblos, south of them, for children and women to be captured and enslaved.

Jicarilla culture was little affected by the agricultural traditions of their captives. Unlike their relatives the Navaho, the Jicarilla remained primarily a hunting people, with their meat diet varied by wild seeds, berries, and fruits which the women gathered.

It would be hard to say with what Indians the Jicarilla were not at war, at one time or another in their history. The southern plains tribes, particularly the Kiowa, Comanche, and Cheyenne, visited the Jicarilla territory to cut spruce and cedar trees to be used as tipi poles. The Jicarilla retaliated by raiding the plains tribes for horses and women.

112

Although, like all hunters, the Jicarilla followed the game, taking elk and moose in the mountains and buffalo and antelope on the plains, the women developed basketry to a fine art. Enormous storage baskets were made to hold gathered plant foods or dried meat; there were basket bowls from which food was eaten, and basket trays on which dice were thrown in gambling games. Even the hunters' canteens were willow baskets coated with piñon gum.

The buffalo origin myth that follows is part of the long saga of the emergence of the people—and the Jicarilla, like the Navaho, call themselves Dené—from the underworld. In its present form the myth is entirely sacred. The Kiowa, who tell the identical myth in a somewhat abbreviated form, identify its hero with their Hero-trickster Saynday, and do not tell it as a part of the sacred cycle of the Twin War Gods, Grandmother Spider, and the Ten Grandmother bundles.

It is probable that the myth's origin is lost somewhere in the Northwest, from which area both Jicarilla and Kiowa probably moved southeastward before the recording of their histories.

▼▼▼▼▼▼

When the people came from the underworld, they traveled southward for four days. During that time they got very hungry, for all they had to eat were the seeds of wild plants. The women made a kind of flour by grinding the seeds between two flat rocks, and a kind of gruel by stirring the flour into water, but still the people were hungry, and they grew tired and weak.

Each night the people camped and rested, and on the fourth night after they left the underworld, one family set its tipi apart from the main camp. The father went with the mother to look for wild seeds, and the children stayed behind to keep up the fire in the tipi.

Pretty soon the children heard somebody strike the side of the tipi, and call to them, "May I come in?"

"Come in," they said, "but we have nothing but water to give you."

"Oh, that's all right," said the stranger, and he walked into the tipi. The stranger was a raven. He had his bow in its case and a quiver full of arrows on his back. He hung them up on the lodge poles as if he lived there and could put his medicine wherever he wanted to. Then the raven turned around and went out, and the children sat and looked at the quiver.

"I wonder what's in it?" the oldest boy said.

"I don't know," answered the oldest girl.

"Let's look and see," suggested the youngest boy.

So the children took the quiver down, and peered inside it. There was a lump of meat and fat.

"What's that, sister?" said the smallest girl.

"Let's taste and try," said the oldest boy.

So he reached into the quiver and pulled out the lump of meat and fat, and tasted it. "It's good," he said. He handed it to the others. All the children ate the meat, and as they ate it they began to get fat. Their mouths were smeared with grease, and even their eyes stuck out with all the good food they had been eating.

Long after dark, the mother came in with her basket of wild seeds. The fire was burning brightly in the tipi, and she could see how much her children had changed since she left them.

"What has happened to you?" the mother cried.

"Look, Mother," said all the children together, and they showed her the lump of meat and fat, which was no larger and no smaller than when the raven left it.

"What is that?" the mother exclaimed.

"Taste it," cried all the children together. "Taste it, Mother. It's good."

So the mother tasted the meat, and she, too, began to grow fat and healthy. She ran out of the tipi to find her husband and tell him about the wonderful thing that had happened. All the people in camp came to see the fat, healthy, beautiful children. They agreed that they would wait to see if the raven came back with more food.

Meantime, Raven knew what had happened. When he found that the food had been stolen from his quiver, he flew away to the east, to a mountain that was too far away for the people to see and find. The bat, who was outside the tipi in the darkness, saw the raven fly away, and followed him. Then she came back and told the people where the raven had gone.

All the people decided to gather in a council and talk things over. "Let us go to Raven's home and find out where he gets that wonderful food," they finally decided.

The people had to travel at night, for the bat was the only guide they had, and she could not see in the daytime. Four nights they traveled, and at last they came to a place in the mountains where there were many ravens. No one could recognize the raven who had visited the people's camp, although they looked and looked for him. The other ravens flew about in great swooping circles, cawing and crying, but saying nothing that the people could understand.

There were a great many logs lying on the ground in that place, pointing in this direction and that. "We should look for logs where there has been a fire," the people decided, and they searched the mountain side, until they found a place where there was a great circle of ashes on the ground. All the ravens cooked together, and left the ashes of a great campfire lying there.

"But where do they get the food they cook?" the people said to one another. And no one could answer.

"Let's lie down in the pine needles and hide and watch," said the war chief. "Then perhaps we can see where the ravens find their food."

All the people sat that night and watched, and the next night, and the next. The ravens flew over their hiding place in great circles, cawing aloud as they swooped and dipped, but they never dropped any food or showed the place where it was hidden.

"Hiding and watching will do us no good," the war chief told the people. "We must try another way."

"What shall we do?" everyone wanted to know.

"Let us call on our medicine man," the war chief decided. "He is the wisest of us all. He will know what to do."

The war chief gave his pipe—his straight pipe, made of a straight piece of cane and wrapped around with sinew—to four of the bravest of his young men. "Take this to our medicine man," he instructed them.

The old medicine man was waiting. The four young men stood before him, and, one after another, three of them offered him the pipe. Each time the medicine man refused, until the fourth young man took the pipe, and closed the medicine man's hands over it. Then he smoked the pipe, once to each of the four corners of the world, once to the Father above, once to the Earth below, and a last puff to the place where he stood and the people all around him.

"Why do you come to me?" the medicine man asked them.

"Father, we have come to you to help us learn where the ravens get their meat," the young men answered.

Again the old man smoked, this time to the four world corners, and then he said, "Very well. I will do what I can to help you. Take me to your chief."

The four young men led the medicine man to the war chief, and when they had smoked together, the medicine man asked, "How can I help you?"

"Use your power to find out for us where the ravens get their food," the war chief replied.

"Very well," said the medicine man. "Who was the first of the people to taste that food?"

"I did," said the oldest boy of the lonely band family.

"Come to me, and do what I tell you to do," said the medicine man, and when the boy stood before him, he used his magic power to turn the boy into a puppy.

"Stay here," the medicine man told him. "The rest of us are going away." The puppy wagged his tail to show that he understood.

Then all the people gathered together whatever they owned, and without making any secret of their movements they left the camp where they had hidden in the pine needles. In the morning, when the ravens saw that the people had gone, they came clustering around the camp, as ravens do, to see what had been left behind.

One little raven boy, looking around and around, suddenly found the puppy. He picked it up in his arms, and ran to his father with it. "Look what I have found," the little boy cried.

"Put it down," his father ordered.

"Throw it away," his mother exclaimed.

"You don't know what kind of dog it is," the parents both said together. "It might be dangerous. Perhaps it has some kind of disease. Get rid of it."

"Please let me keep it," the little boy begged, and he began to cry. "It's a pretty puppy. Look. He's trying to talk to me with his eyes."

"Perhaps he's trying to put a curse on you!" the mother screamed. "Don't have anything to do with that thing! Throw it away, I tell you!"

But the little boy begged and pleaded. He was their only child, and his parents could hardly stand to see him so sad.

"I tell you what," said the father finally. "I'll pass a blazing stick in front of his eyes. If he doesn't cry, or turn away, then you can keep him. But one yip out of that puppy, and away he goes!"

The father seized a blazing stick from the fire, and passed it in front of the puppy's eyes. Of course the little boy had understood everything the raven said, so he stared back at the flame without making a sound.

"All right," agreed the raven father then. "If he can do that, you can keep him."

The little boy and the puppy snuggled down happily in their

buffalo robes that night. The puppy had never before felt anything so warm and soft.

The little raven and his new pet played happily all the next day. Late in the evening, they went back into the raven tipi. "It's suppertime," the mother said.

"All right," answered the father, and he brushed the ashes away from the fireplace. A great flat stone lay there. The raven lifted the stone, and disappeared beneath it. Presently he came back, driving a buffalo before him. He killed the buffalo with his stone knife, and all the ravens gathered for the feast.

Every day for three days the same thing happened. The father raven brought a buffalo out of the earth beneath the fireplace stone. On the fourth morning, the boy of the People decided that he could do the same thing.

He waited until the sun was high in the sky and all the ravens were busy outside the tipi, in their camp. Then he turned himself back into a boy, and took a white eagle feather in his right hand. With his magic feather, the boy pushed away the fireplace stone, and descended into the hole in the earth which it had covered.

Down below there was a beautiful world, green with grass, with lakes of blue water scattered here and there. Many animals were grazing, and there were great herds of buffalo of many colors. Four of them seemed to be the chiefs.

The boy took his eagle feather, and went up to the first buffalo, which was white. He put the white feather in the white buffalo's mouth. The buffalo shook his head.

"That is not for me," said the white buffalo. "Take it to my brother." He jerked his head in the direction of the black buffalo chief.

The boy went to the black buffalo chief, and placed the feather in his mouth, but the buffalo shook his head.

"That is not for me," he said, "Go back to my brother. He really is the greatest of all the animals."

So the boy took the feather back, and returned to the white buffalo. "I know your power now," he said. "You are really the chief of all the animals—their leader, and the most sacred of them all." The buffalo held the feather in his mouth, and followed the boy to the surface of the earth. All the other animals, of every kind, followed them. That is why the hide of a white buffalo is sacred, and must be used in many ceremonies.

By the time the boy of the people and the animals came through the hole, it was night, and the ravens were asleep. One of them heard the animals pass, and jumped to his feet, wide awake. He tried to push back the stone over the hole but he was too late; the animals were gone.

"Well, you have won over us," the raven said. "The animals belong to the people now. But whenever you kill any game, you must leave the eyes for the ravens to eat." And so it has been done ever since.

The boy found the track the people had left, and, with the animals following him, set out to find his family. He came to the first place where the people had camped, and there he found an old firestick someone had forgotten, lying beside the cold camp fire ashes.

"Which way did my people go?" the boy asked the firestick. "When did they leave here?"

"They traveled west, back to the mountains," the firestick replied. "They left here three days ago."

The next morning the boy and the animals started on, and in the evening they came to another deserted campsite. Here they found an old ladder someone had left behind.

"When did my people leave here?" the boy asked the ladder.

"Two days ago," the ladder answered. "You are following close on their trail."

At the third camping place, the following night, the boy found another old firestick, and when he asked it how far away the people were, the firestick answered, "They left here yesterday."

The fourth night they found another old ladder. "Oh, the people left here early this morning," the ladder said when the boy questioned it. "Hurry along on your way. You'll catch up with them."

And so it was. On the fifth evening the boy, with his animals following him as tamely as if they were sheep, walked into the people's camp. The buffalo scattered out, and all the animals began to graze wherever they could find food.

One of the deer went to the lodge of an old woman who lived all alone, and began to nibble the brush that covered her shelter. The old woman was angry, because it had taken her a lot of time and trouble to build even her little brush hut. She caught up a stick from the fire, and rushed outside, where she began to beat the deer over the nose. The white ashes on the stick stuck to the deer's nose, and from that day to this, every deer has carried a white mark across its face.

"Stay away from the people from now on," the old woman ordered. "Your nose will tell you when you are getting near them."

The deer left the camp, and all the other animals followed him, for they would not stay in a place where their brother was mistreated. And from that day to this, animals will come near a camp only at night, and the people must search far and wide for game in the day-time. Men and animals were no longer friends, and because of the old woman, the animals could smell the people and stay far away from them.

▼▼▼▼▼

Retold from: Russell, Frank, "Myths of the Jicarilla Apache," *Journal of American Folklore, Vol. XI, No. xl (January–March, 1898), pp. 253–271.*

To Feed My People:
The Race Between
the Buffalo and Man

Once again we turn to the Cheyenne of the central plains for a story of how the buffalo became the food of man. As one might expect with the fighting Cheyenne, this is the story of a contest, in which the buffalo woman is finally defeated by the hawk man. It was an equal contest, however, and the victory was fairly won.

Long, long ago, when Maheo had made the world and set the men and animals upon it, everybody was equal. Men and animals alike lived on Maheo's earth, and all enjoyed it.

Presently, though, the buffalo began talking among themselves.

"We are the biggest animals in the whole world," the buffalo chief said. "Why should we let the others be equal to us? They should honor and respect us, as is our due."

"You're right," said the buffalo young men. "Everybody can see how big and strong we are. Why, right now, men act as if they had as much power as we do."

"The weakest of our women is stronger than any man," the

120

buffalo chief agreed. "Let us go and talk to them, and show them that they must be our servants, not our equals."

It was Sun Dance time, and the people were camped in the great circle around the Sun Dance lodge. The buffalo chief led his people in from the east, and walked straight to the lodge door. There he stood, facing the Sun Dance priest who sat on the west side of the lodge, behind the altar.

"Come in and be welcome," the Sun Dance priest said.

"Why should we be asked to come in?" the buffalo chief demanded.

"Because all our friends are welcome to watch our dance, and to share in it," the Sun Dance priest replied.

"We are not here as your friends, to share in anything," the buffalo chief responded. "We are here as your masters, to tell you that we are the strongest people in the world."

"All beings are friends, Maheo taught us that," said the Sun Dance priest.

"We will prove it to you," sneered the buffalo chief. "We will run a race; the weakest of our women against any men you please."

"Let us make a fair race, if race we must," the Sun Dance priest said. "My young men have been starving and thirsting and dancing for four days now. They are weak. Let us have a relay race, with four runners on each side. Let the other animals, and the birds, choose which team they will be on."

The buffalo chief looked around at his young men. "What do you think of this man's plan?" he asked them.

"Hah!" they all said. "It is fair. Let it be so."

"Send out the runners," the buffalo chief commanded. "Call all the animals and birds together, and let them decide on which side they will run."

So the runners went out, east and south and west and north, and carried the word of the Great Race to all the animals and birds they could find. The fishes and the turtles would not come, because the race was to be run on dry land, and so they could not take part.

At the end of four days, all the birds and animals had gathered in the Sun Dance camp, and pitched their tipis in a second great circle around it. On the morning of the fifth day they gathered at the Sun Dance lodge, to choose their sides.

The buffalo had planned to run alone, but to their surprise other animals joined them. The elk came to the buffalo's team, and so did the deer and the antelope. All the fast animals with split hooves were on one team.

"Now, who will run with us?" the Sun Dance priest called.

"I will," said the dog. "I live in the people's camps, and they are my friends. I will run with you."

"Who else?" asked the Sun Dance priest.

"I will," said the youngest man of all the Sun Dancers. "I am not tired; my sacrifice has given me strength. I will run for my own people."

"And I," said the eagle, "for you honor me by using my feathers in your sacred ceremonies. I will run for you."

"I will run for the same reason," said the hawk. "The people have always used my feathers in their prayer fans and I will run for them."

So the Sun Dance priest and the buffalo chief laid out the race course, from the Devil's Tower in North Dakota to the Teton Mountains in Wyoming, and they stationed the runners along it. The young Sun Dancer was paired with the elk; the dog was paired with the deer; the antelope was paired with the eagle, and the hawk was paired with the buffalo woman.

Everybody had to laugh when the buffalo woman came out; she looked so funny. Her head was big, and her hair was as shaggy as if she had never combed it. Her shoulders were wide, but her waist was tiny and narrow, and her legs were so thin she looked as if she could never run on them. Around her waist she wore a little fuzzy apron, that looked as if it were made from the same shaggy hair she wore on her head.

Beside her, the prairie falcon looked trim and straight, but very small. He held his wings folded close to his sides, and he did not spread them at all.

The Sun Dance priest and the buffalo chief stood side by side at the starting line. When they were ready, they hit the drum with one hard blow, and the first pair of runners were off. The young Sun Dancer ran hard and fast, but he could not keep up with the elk, and when the dog and the deer started, the dog was already behind. He did his best, but he could hardly gain on the deer, and when the antelope and eagle began their course, the antelope was far ahead. But the eagle was strong, if not as fast as the antelope, and the antelope began to get tired and drop behind long before the eagle did. When they came to the buffalo woman and the hawk they were neck and neck again, as the first runners had been at the beginning.

Oh, how fast Buffalo Woman could run on those skinny legs of hers! She was young and she was quick, and she was running for the honor of her own people. The prairie falcon spread his great wings and rose from the ground so easily that it looked as if he would be slow. But as he soared along, using all the wind currents to carry him and hardly seeming to move his wings, he was still even with Buffalo Woman, and he was saving all his strength.

At last they saw the Tetons standing white-topped and beautiful before them. Buffalo Woman ran as fast as she could, but now the hawk began to move his wings and really fly. He was sitting on the highest mountain top when Buffalo Woman stumbled to her tired knees at its foot.

All the people and all the animals had gathered in a great camp to watch the finish of the race, and now the men and their friends sent up the victory call for the hawk, who floated lazily down the mountain side to receive his new war honors. The buffalo and the split-hoof animals broke their camp and went away without speaking, for they knew they would never be the equals of the men and the birds again.

Many things came out of the Great Race. In the first place, the split hooves became the game animals which men hunted for food and clothing and shelter. In the second place, the hawk became known as the greatest of all birds, greater even than the eagle. And in the hawk's honor the Cheyennes set up the first and greatest of the soldier societies: the Hawk Soldiers. Only ten men, the bravest of the brave, could be Hawk Soldiers, and it was their honor to stake themselves to the ground in battle and to fight to the death unless their brothers released them.

▼▼▼▼▼▼

Told to Alice Marriott by Mary Little Bear Inkanish and by John Fletcher.

How and Why:
The Painted Turtle

In every Indian tribe there are "little stories," or "how and why" stories. These explain natural phenomena, usually in terms of the actions of the Culture Hero, the Trickster, or that undeniably Indian combination of the two characters, the Hero-Trickster.

It is often difficult to separate these personalities, especially when the original stories have been overlaid with Christian elements, or with bits and pieces of pre-Christian European folklore. An endless battle rages in the pages of learned journals about the relationship between Indian "how and why" stories and the Uncle Remus tales of the Negro South, which are of African origin.

In the story that follows, which is evidently a compilation of many tales that had been told the teller, European influence is clear and unmistakable.

▼▼▼▼▼

Once upon a time, the people lived in a village near a big lake. It was a beautiful village, with high trees around to give it shade, and the women went out every morning and swept the ground to keep it clean and neat.

In the cleanest house in the whole village, Jesus lived with his grandmother. People say that he was sent to earth to teach everyone how to do good, and the right way to live. And his grandmother was just like him. She was a fine old lady, always helping people who were in need, and teaching the younger women the things a woman needs to know.

In a house across the village, the soft-shell turtle lived by himself. He didn't have a wife; he was a ladies' man who flirted with every woman who would look at him. He took girls away from their sweethearts and wives away from their husbands, and made trouble for everybody.

Finally the village was in such an uproar that Jesus' grandmother said to him, "Jesus, you've got to do something about that turtle. Nobody can get anything done because of him. The men don't want to go hunting because they're afraid to leave their wives in the village with him, and the women won't go out to gather rushes for mats, or wild plants for food, because they're afraid of him. Now you were sent here so the people could live happily and at peace with one another, and you've got to do something about that troublemaker."

"All right," Jesus said, "I will."

He turned himself into a beautiful young woman, with long, thick black hair and big dark eyes. He took a wooden bowl full of corn soup his grandmother had standing by the fire, and walked across the village to the turtle's house.

"Here I am," Jesus called in the soft voice of a young girl. "I've brought you a present."

"Come on in," said the turtle, and Jesus-woman lifted the mat hanging over the door and stepped inside the mat-covered house.

Turtle was sitting on his bed, leaning back against a log, and he was painting his face. He put a red dot on each cheek and a red dot on his forehead. He parted his hair down the middle with a maple-wood stick, and painted the parting red. Then he spit in the fire, and the spittle turned into pearls and diamonds.

"Pick them up," said Turtle, indifferently. "There are plenty more where those came from."

Jesus-woman gathered up the jewels. Turtle painted a red line around one leg, and then he spat in the fire again. While Jesus-woman was gathering up those jewels, Turtle painted a red line around the other leg. Then he spat again.

"You can have those, too," Turtle said. "And if you want to

come for a walk with me in the woods, I'll give you something better yet.''

"I don't know whether I ought to walk in the woods with any-body," Jesus-woman said. "My grandmother told me that's the way girls get into trouble.''

"Look at me," Turtle commanded. "Don't you think I'm hand-some? Don't you like the way I'm painted? Do you think such a fine man as I am would get a girl into trouble?''

"Well, I don't know," said Jesus-woman, turning the jewels over and over in her hands.

"Oh, come on," Turtle insisted. Now he really wanted that girl. "I'll show you all sorts of things.''

"All right," Jesus-woman said, and she followed him out of the wickiup and into the woods. They walked a long way, until they came to a clearing. The trees roofed it over like a summer house.

"Here we are," said Turtle, and he sat down with his back lean-ing against a tree. "Come and sit beside me, my little sweetheart.''

Jesus-woman sat beside Turtle, and Turtle put his arm around her.

"Isn't this nice?" asked Turtle. He slid down along the ground, until he was lying flat. "Come on, lie down beside me, my little dear.''

Jesus-woman lay down beside Turtle. Pretty soon Turtle closed his eyes. Jesus-woman had used her magic to put a spell on him, and soon he was drowsy and soon after that he was asleep.

Then Jesus-woman got up. She found a rotten log in the under-brush at the side of the clearing. The log was alive and crawling with red ants, the kind that can kill you if you get enough bites from them. Jesus-woman rolled the log over to Turtle, and Turtle sleepily put his arms around it and drew the log close to him.

Pretty soon the ants woke up and began to crawl all over Turtle's body. "Don't do that," said Turtle, shifting around. "You tickle.''

But the ants kept on crawling on him, and Turtle got more and more uncomfortable. "Lie still," he ordered. "You can't find out about what I brought you here for if you keep on tickling.''

Finally the ants were angry enough to begin to bite him. Turtle sat up, and threw the log away from him. Then he looked up, and before Turtle's eyes Jesus-woman changed back to his own form.

"Now," he said, "you've made enough trouble for all the people. You've upset the village long enough. From now on, people will know what you are because with all your fancy paint you'll crawl around on your belly. And I'll leave the paint on you, too, so that everyone will always recognize you.''

This story is to be told to young men, as a warning of what may happen to them if they act like turtles.

▾▾▾▾▾▾

Told to Carol K. Rachlin by Bertha Manitowa Dowd and Lorena Manitowa.

How and Why:
Why the Bear Waddles
When He Walks

COMANCHE

Uniquely, among the Plains tribes, the Comanches seem to have had neither fear of nor respect for the bear as an animal possessing supernatural powers. While the Kiowa fear of bears was so strong that they would not speak the word, unless it was part of a name won on the vision quest, and always used a synonym to refer to it, the Comanches had one word and one word only which meant bear. While the Cheyennes and Arapahos thought of the bears as their ancestors, and believed they were capable of sexual intercourse with human beings, so that to eat a bear was an act of cannibalism, those "aboriginal skeptics" the Comanches found bear very good eating whenever they could hunt it down.

The "hand game" referred to in the following story is a glorified form of button-button-who's-got-the-button, which is found in some form everywhere among North American Indians. In playing the game, two people hold two counters, one marked and one unmarked, in either hand. The guesser for the opposing team tries to find both marked counters in a single guess. If he succeeds, the counters pass to

128

his side. If he fails, they remain with the original team. The writers have taken part in hand games which began in the morning and lasted until dark.

During the hand game drummers and singers try to confuse the guessers with their music. The losing side dances in honor of the other. Plains Indians do not play hand game in summer, when the snakes are out, only in winter.

▼▼▼▼▼▼

In the beginning days, nobody knew what to do with the sun. It would come up and shine for a long time. Then it would go away for a long time, and everything would be dark.

The daytime animals naturally wanted the sun to shine all the time, so they could live their lives without being interrupted by the dark. The nighttime animals wanted the sun to go away forever, so they could live the way they wanted to.

At last they all got together, to talk things over.

Old Man Coyote said, "Let's see what we can do about that sun. One of us ought to have it, or the other side ought to get rid of it."

"How will we do that?" Scissor-tailed Flycatcher asked. "Nobody can tell the sun what to do. He's more powerful than anyone else in the world."

"Why don't we play hand game for it?" Bear asked. "The winning side can keep the sun or throw it away, depending on who wins and what they want to do with it."

So they got out the guessing bones to hide in their hands, and they got out the crow-feathered wands for the guessers to point with, and they got out the twenty painted dogwood sticks for the umpires to keep score with. Coyote was the umpire for the day side, and nighttime umpire was Owl.

The umpires got a flat rock, like a table, and laid out their counting sticks on that. Then the two teams brought logs, and lined them up facing one another, with the umpires and their flat rock at one end, between the two teams.

That was a long hand game. The day side held the bones first, and they were so quick and skillful passing them from hand to hand behind their backs and waving them in the guessers' faces that it seemed surely they must win. Then Mole, who was guessing for the night side, caught both Scissor-tail and Hawk at the same time, and the bones went to the night side, and the day people began to guess.

Time and again the luck went back and forth, each team seeming to be about to beat the other. Time and again the luck changed, and the winning team became the losing one.

The game went on and on. Finally the sun, waiting on the other side of the world to find out what was going to happen to him, got tired of it all.

The game was so long that Bear got tired, too. He was playing on the night side. He got cramped sitting on the log, and his legs began to ache. Bear took off his moccasins to rest his feet, and still the game went on and on.

At last the sun was so bored that he decided to go and see for himself what was happening. He yawned and stretched and crawled out of his bed on the underneath side of the world. He started to climb up his notched log ladder to the top side, to find out what was happening.

As the sun climbed the light grew stronger, and the night people began to be afraid. The game was still even; nobody had won. But the sun was coming and coming, and the night animals had to run away. Bear jumped up in such a hurry that he put his right foot in his left moccasin, and his left foot in his right moccasin.

The sun was full up now, and all the other night animals were gone. Bear went after them as fast as he could in his wrong moccasins, rocking and waddling from side to side, and shouting, "Wait for me! Wait for me!"

But nobody stopped or waited, and Bear had to go waddling along, just the way he has done ever since.

And because nobody won the game, the day and night took turns from that time on. Everybody had the same time to come out and live his life the way he wanted to as everybody else.

▼▼▼▼▼▼

Told to Carol K. Rachlin by Marie Cox.

How and Why:
Don't Be Greedy Story

The "little stories" were told to amuse and instruct children. Sometimes, like the hand game for the sun story which has just been told, the little stories explained natural phenomena. Sometimes, as in the story that follows, they are lessons in behavior.

True to Comanche form, we find the owl, which was dreaded as an omen of death or a restless spirit returned, figuring in this story as a semicomic being who outtricks the Trickster, Coyote.

Old Man Coyote, he was the one who was always getting in trouble. All the time, whatever he did, he couldn't stay out of it.

Old Man Coyote, he was the one who was always curious about what other people were doing. Whenever he saw somebody doing something Old Man Coyote wanted to imitate it. That was one reason he got into trouble all the time.

One evening, Old Man Coyote was walking along, walking along, and he came to an elm tree where an owl was sitting. The owl was doing something Old Man Coyote never saw before. First he would put up his claw and pull his right eye out of its socket, and toss it up

131

in the air. Then he would hold out his claw. The eye dropped back in place in his head, and his hand was all filled with good sweet dried meat. Then the owl would do the same thing with his left eye.

Old Man Coyote, he stood and watched what the owl was doing. Old Man Coyote was always hungry, always greedy. After a while he said, "Owl, what are you doing there?"

"Oh," answered Owl, "this is the way I get my food, out of the air." That was true, because the owl eats smaller birds, or he swoops down upon little animals, like the rabbits and the wood mice.

"Can anybody do it?" Coyote asked.

"No," said Owl, "just the ones that know how. You have to have this kind of power."

Coyote watched some more. Getting food that way looked so eeeeeasy! If that silly owl can do it, Old Man Coyote thought, surely, with all my brains, I can do it too.

So Old Man Coyote waited until Owl had his head turned upward for his eye to fall into place, and he pulled his own right eye out of its socket. He threw the eye up in the air, and stood with his hand out, waiting for his eye to come back in its place, and the dried meat to light on his palm.

Nothing happened. The eye caught on a branch of the elm tree, and there was no dried meat in his hand. Old Man Coyote was sure mad!

"I'll get you down," he scolded at his eye. "I'll make you sorry for the way you acted!" He pulled his left eye out of its socket, and tossed it upward. "Go and find your brother," he ordered. "Make him come home. Both of you bring me some dried meat right away!"

But the left eye caught on the tree, too, and Old Man Coyote was left standing under the tree with his hands held out, while the owl ate up his eyes. Then Old Man Coyote was left to crawl around and around the tree on the ground, yelling for his eyes to come back.

That's the end of that story.

▼▼▼▼▼

Told to Alice Marriott and Carol K. Rachlin by Marie Cox.

How Horses Came to the Navaho

NAVAHO

*The Navaho, like the other southern Athabascans, have many tradi-
tions and legends of how, when, and where they received the horses,
donkeys, cattle, and sheep which eventually became their main depen-
dence. The story that follows is only one of the many, and is chosen
because its chief character, the Gambler, personifies many Navaho
personality traits.*

A long time ago, when the Navaho were poor, and lived by hunting
and gathering wild seeds and plants, they used to have to hunt for
ways to amuse themselves. Sometimes they ran foot races. Sometimes
the young men climbed trees to see who could go the highest. And
sometimes they played the moccasin game, hiding a nut or a bone in
one of a pair of moccasins, and then trying to guess which shoe held
the counter.

Well, there was one man who would bet on anything. He was such
a gambler that the people called him Gambler. He would bet his moccasins, his clothes, his weapons, even his wives. Sometimes he won and
sometimes he lost, but most times he came out about even, like everybody else.

One day the Gambler met a man who said to him, "I hear you like
to play the moccasin game."

"Very much," the Gambler answered.

"Let us play," the stranger said. "What will you bet me first?"

Gambler had been very lucky up to that time. He had traveled east, to the village Indians of the Rio Grande, and had won strings of white shell beads and brown shell beads and turquoise beads and jet beads. He had won the little carved blue stone figures that bring hunters luck, and he had won four new wives. They were very young and very beautiful. Each one had her own grinding stones, and they were hard workers, turning wild seeds into flour almost before you saw them move.

So Gambler looked at his fine new possessions, and he thought a moment. Then he said, "I'll bet you a string of shell beads. Which one do you want?"

"Let's play for the white shell beads," said his enemy. "I'll bet you my new high moccasins with the turned-up toes against that string of beads."

Gambler got a little uneasy then, because he knew that the Jicarilla Apache wore that kind of moccasins, and they were great gamblers.

It was early in the morning when they started playing, sitting in the shade on the west side of a piñon tree. By noon Gambler had lost all his shell beads, and his turquoise beads and his jet beads. He said to the Jicarilla man, "Let's stop a while and eat. My wives will prepare food for us."

"All right," said the Jicarilla man. "We'll have some lunch. I'm hungry too. Then I'll play you for that blue stone figure that brings a man luck."

"No," said Gambler. "I won't play you for that. I want that more than anything. As long as I have it, I'll beat you yet."

"Oh, all right," said the Jicarilla.

The four new wives got busy, and almost before the Jicarilla had stored his winnings away in his pouch, they had lunch ready. The men sat down and ate, while the women waited on them.

"This is good food," said the Jicarilla. "I'll play you for your wives."

"One at a time," said Gambler.

"Oh, certainly, one at a time," the Jicarilla agreed. "It's getting warm here, though. Let's move around to the shade on the east side of the tree." When they had moved, the Jicarilla took off his short bow, built of layers of deer sinew pasted one after another to a shaft of mountain mahogany. He laid his spotted-bobcat quiver full of dogwood arrows on the ground beside him. "Weapons make a man hot, when he wears them while he's gambling," the Jicarilla said.

One after another, Gambler bet his four wives against the Jicarilla's weapons. One after another, he lost the women, and the bow and quiver full of arrows remained on the ground by the Jicarilla's side. At last Gambler had nothing left in the world except his hunting fetish.

"Now you'll have to bet that turquoise luck piece," said the Jicarilla. "I don't think it's worth much, to tell you the truth. It hasn't brought you any luck today."

Gambler sighed. It was nearly dark. The sun had gone down and the sunset light had almost gone. The day was nearly over, and he had won nothing.

"All right," he said. "I'll bet my hunting fetish against your bow and arrows. The things go together anyway."

They played once more, and Gambler lost. The Jicarilla man took up his bow and nocked an arrow to the string. "I'll see that you don't get any of them back, too," he said, and shot straight at Gambler.

The arrow carried him up, up, up, above the sky, to the world where it was always light. There he saw the Creator sitting, almost as if he were waiting for him.

"Sit down," the Creator said.

"Why do you ask me to sit down?" Gambler asked. "I am a poor man now. I lost everything I had to that Jicarilla."

"Don't worry," the Creator said. "Sit down and rest and eat. Here is food. When you feel better, I will tell you something."

Gambler ate the food that was set before him, and he felt stronger than he ever had in his life. Then the Creator said, "Now you will be poor no longer. Look over there to the south. What do you see?"

Gambler, stretching and straining his eyes, looked far and away to the south. There he saw people—many people. He saw, too, animals such as he had never seen before: horses and burros, cattle, sheep, fowls, and cats.

"What are these?" he asked the Creator.

"Those are the Mexicans," the Creator told him. "They and all their animals shall be yours, and you will be like a god to them. Be kind to your people and their beasts, and treat them well. Perhaps someday you will lead them north again, but now you must go south and care for them."

Before Gambler knew what had happened, he stood on the ground among the people of the south. They marveled at the way he had appeared among them.

"You must be a god," said the oldest and wisest of the Mexican men. "We will give you a new name, to show how great you are, and how different you are from other people. We will call you Moctezuma."

So for many years Moctezuma, the Gambler, lived in Mexico, among his new people. He was very busy taking care of them, but sometimes his heart ached, and he yearned for the northern country where he used to live. At last he called his councilors and warriors around him.

"Come with me," he said, "and we will go to another country. I will show you the place where I was born, and the people of my heart. We will bring them all these new animals, for they have none of these creatures. We will teach my people what we know, and they in turn will teach us."

And so it was. They formed a great caravan and traveled northward, to the Rio Grande. On the way they passed a great stone, shaped like a throne, and Moctezuma said, "I will sit here and rest a moment. Then we will go on."

He sat and rested for a while on the great thronelike rock that the Hopis, to this day, call Moctezuma's chair.

"No other person should ever rest there, for it is a holy place," said the oldest and wisest men. Moctezuma created rattlesnakes and filled his throne with them, and there they still are. No human being dares go near that throne except in the dead of winter. Even then Moctezuma's rattlesnakes will stir and whir their buttoned tails in warning.

Then Moctezuma and the Mexicans went on, and in time they came to the Rio Grande. There the fields were fertile and the grass grew thick for pasture. There the Mexicans built their first village, at the place where the Rio Chama flows into the Rio Grande, and there the Mexicans began to teach the northern Indians the things they knew.

Now Moctezuma's work was finished. The Creator called to him and he went away, up, up, up to the world above the sky. There Moctezuma waits, until his people need him again.

▼▼▼▼▼

This is combined from two sources, each equally accurate. The story of the Gambler who became Moctezuma, and who brought his people horses from the south was told by Hasteen Klah, Navaho medicine

man and weaver, to the late Mary Cabot Wheelwright, who in turn
told it to Alice Marriott. The story of Moctezuma's throne, in
Coconino County, Arizona, was told by David Taliweftema, Hopi,
to Alice Marriott, with the comment, "This is part of a longer
story, but it is the only part that is safe to tell you because the
rest is much too sacred. Some day maybe I will tell you the rest."

Certainly, observable facts support the statement that Moctezuma set rattlesnakes to guard his throne. A large ruin stands
nearby, but has never been excavated because of the density of the
rattlesnake population. Even the Hopi snake priests, collecting
snakes for their summer dance, avoid the place—perhaps because
the God of the Mexicans once sat there.

The End of the World:
The Buffalo Go

And now we come to the end of a world. The end of the buffalo was the end of Plains Indian life. And before the white man's superior technology, the buffalo succumbed. This is one story of why there are no more buffalo in the world.

Everything the Kiowas had came from the buffalo. Their tipis were made of buffalo hides, so were their clothes and moccasins. They ate buffalo meat. Their containers were made of hide, or of bladders or stomachs. The buffalo were the life of the Kiowas.

Most of all, the buffalo was part of the Kiowa religion. A white buffalo calf must be sacrificed in the Sun Dance. The priests used parts of the buffalo to make their prayers when they healed people or when they sang to the powers above.

So, when the white men wanted to build railroads, or when they wanted to farm or raise cattle, the buffalo still protected the Kiowas. They tore up the railroad tracks and the gardens. They chased the cattle off the ranges. The buffalo loved their people as much as the Kiowas loved them.

138

There was war between the buffalo and the white men. The white men built forts in the Kiowa country, and the woolly-headed buffalo soldiers [the Tenth Cavalry, made up of Negro troops] shot the buffalo as fast as they could, but the buffalo kept coming on, coming on, even into the post cemetery at Fort Sill. Soldiers were not enough to hold them back.

Then the white men hired hunters to do nothing but kill the buffalo. Up and down the plains those men ranged, shooting sometimes as many as a hundred buffalo a day. Behind them came the skinners with their wagons. They piled the hides and bones into the wagons until they were full, and then took their loads to the new railroad stations that were being built, to be shipped east to the market. Sometimes there would be a pile of bones as high as a man, stretching a mile along the railroad track.

The buffalo saw that their day was over. They could protect their people no longer. Sadly, the last remnant of the great herd gathered in council, and decided what they would do.

The Kiowas were camped on the north side of Mount Scott, those of them who were still free to camp. One young woman got up very early in the morning. The dawn mist was still rising from Medicine Creek, and as she looked across the water, peering through the haze, she saw the last buffalo herd appear like a spirit dream.

Straight to Mount Scott the leader of the herd walked. Behind him came the cows and their calves, and the few young males who had survived. As the woman watched, the face of the mountain opened.

Inside Mount Scott the world was green and fresh, as it had been when she was a small girl. The rivers ran clear, not red. The wild plums were in blossom, chasing the red buds up the inside slopes. Into this world of beauty the buffalo walked, never to be seen again.

Told to Alice Marriott by Old Lady Horse (Spear Woman), Kiowa.

Unpainted, unpolished rain god from Tesuque Pueblo, New Mexico.

Painted rain god from Tesuque Pueblo.

Hopi rabbit kachina, made by Tewaqueptew, a Sun Chief, Old Oraibi, Arizona.

Hopi-carved "Navaho" tablita kachina. The tablita kachina is given to each child at the first dance after his birth and is hung on his cradle.

Ojibway beaded cuff, c. 1890.

Ponca beaded purse, 1937.

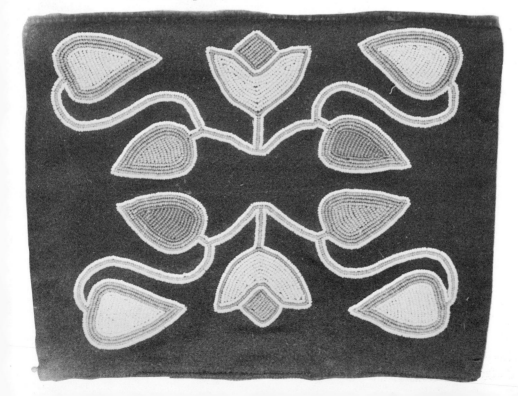

Cheyenne pipe bag and "cloud blower" pipe. The pipe is made from a deer tibia. (*Dr. Harry L. Deupree collection*)

Man's beaded "dance apron," worn to replace old-fashioned breech clout. Probably Kiowa, c. 1910. (*Dr. Harry L. Deupree collection*)

Water jar from Laguna Pueblo, New Mexico, c. 1750.

Bowl from Sitkyatki Site, Arizona, c. A.D. 850, shows Kokopelli, the hump-backed flute player. Kokopelli was supposed to have brought the harvest and happiness to the Hopi. (*Florence Hollenback collection*)

Part Three
THE WORLD WE LIVE IN NOW

Saynday and Smallpox:
The White Man's Gift

KIOWA

Saynday is the Trickster-Hero of the Kiowas. In this story he appears in his heroic aspect, protecting his people and turning destruction against their traditional enemies, the Pawnees.

This particular legend dates from the late nineteenth century, as its context shows. It is an example of the persistence of old patterns, for Saynday stories are still being made and told, with the character fitting himself into twentieth-century life.

Like all Saynday stories, this one begins:

▼▼▼▼▼▼

Saynday was coming along, and as he came he saw that all his world had changed. Where the buffalo herds used to graze, he saw white-faced cattle. The Washita River, which once ran bankful with clear water, was soggy with red mud. There were no deer or antelope in the brush or skittering across the high plains. No white tipis rose proudly against the blue sky; settlers' soddies dented the hillsides and the creek banks.

143

My time has come, Saynday thought to himself. The world I lived in is dead. Soon the Kiowa people will be fenced like the white man's cattle, and they cannot break out of the fences because the barbed wire will tear their flesh. I can't help my people any longer by staying with them. My time has come, and I will have to go away from this changed world.

Off across the prairie, Saynday saw a dark spot coming toward him from the east, moving very slowly.

That's strange, too, Saynday thought to himself. The East is the place of birth and of new life. The things that come from the East come quickly; they come dancing and alive. This thing comes as slowly as death to an old man. I wonder what it is?

Almost absent-mindedly, Saynday started walking eastward. As he went the spot grew larger, and after a while Saynday saw that it was a man on a horse.

The horse was black, but it had been powdered to roan with the red dust that the plows had stirred up when they slashed open the plains. Red dust spotted the man's clothing—a black suit and a high hat, like a missionary's. Red dust blurred his features, but behind the dust Saynday could see that the man's face was pitted with terrible scars.

The stranger drew rein, and sat looking at Saynday. The black roan horse lifted one sore hoof and drooped its head as if it were too weary to carry its burden any farther.

"Who are you?" the stranger asked.

"I'm Saynday. I'm the Kiowas' Old Uncle Saynday. I'm the one who's always coming along."

"I never heard of you," the stranger said, "and I never heard of the Kiowas. Who are they?"

"The Kiowas are my people," Saynday said, and even in that hard time he stood up proudly, like a man. "Who are you?"

"I'm Smallpox," the man answered.

"And I never heard of *you*," said Saynday. "Where do you come from and what do you do and why are you here?"

"I come from far away, across the Eastern Ocean," Smallpox answered. "I am one with the white men—they are my people as the Kiowas are yours. Sometimes I travel ahead of them, and sometimes I lurk behind. But I am always their companion and you will find me in their camps and in their houses."

"What do you do?" Saynday repeated.

"I bring death," Smallpox replied. "My breath causes children to wither like young plants in spring snow. I bring destruction. No matter how beautiful a woman is, once she has looked at me she becomes as ugly as death. And to men I bring not death alone, but the destruction of their children and the blighting of their wives. The strongest warriors go down before me. No people who have looked on me will ever be the same.'' And he chuckled low and hideously. With his raised forearm, Smallpox pushed the dust off his face, and Saynday saw the scars that disfigured it.

For a moment Saynday shut his eyes against the sight, and then he opened them again. ''Does that happen to all the people you visit?'' he inquired.

''Every one of them,'' said Smallpox. ''It will happen to your Kiowa people, too. Where do they live? Take me to them, and then I will spare you, although you have seen my face. If you do not lead me to your people, I will breathe on you and you will die, no matter whose Old Uncle you are.'' And although he did not breathe on Saynday, Saynday smelled the reek of death that surrounded him.

''My Kiowa people are few and poor already,'' Saynday said, thinking fast as he talked. ''They aren't worth your time and trouble.''

''I have time and I don't have to take any trouble,'' Smallpox told him. ''Even one person whom I blot out, I can count.''

''Oh,'' said Saynday. ''Some of your ways are like the Kiowas', then. You count the enemies that you touch.''

''I have no enemies,'' said Smallpox. ''Man, woman, or child —humanity is all alike to me. I was brought here to kill. But, yes, I count those I destroy. White men always count: cattle, sheep, chickens, children, the living and the dead. You say the Kiowas do the same thing?''

''Only the enemies they touch,'' Saynday insisted. ''They never count living people—men are not cattle, any more than women and children are.''

''Then how do you know the Kiowas are so few and poor?'' Smallpox demanded.

''Oh, anybody can see that for himself,'' Saynday said. ''You can look at a Kiowa camp and tell how small it is. We're not like the Pawnees. They have great houses, half underground, in big villages by the rivers, and every house is full of people.''

''I like that,'' Smallpox observed. ''I can do my best work when people are crowded together.''

''Then you'd like the Pawnees,'' Saynday assured him. ''They're the ones that almost wiped out the Kiowas; that's why we're so few and so poor. Now we run away whenever we see a stranger coming, because he might be a Pawnee.''

"I suppose the Pawnees never run away," Smallpox sneered.

"They couldn't if they wanted to," Saynday replied. "The Pawnees are rich. They have piles of robes, they have lots of cooking pots and plenty of bedding—they keep all kinds of things in those underground houses of theirs. The Pawnees can't run away and leave all their wealth."

"Where did you say they live?" Smallpox asked thoughtfully.

"Oh, over there," Saynday said, jerking his chin to the north.

"And they are rich, and live in houses, with piles of robes to creep into and hide?"

"That's the Pawnees," Saynday said jauntily. He began to feel better. The deathly smell was not so strong now. "I think I'll go and visit the Pawnees first," Smallpox remarked. "Later on, perhaps, I can get back to the Kiowas."

"You do that," directed Saynday. "Go and visit the Pawnees, and when you grow tired there from all the work you have to do, come back and visit my poor people. They'll do all they can for you."

"Good," said Smallpox. He picked up his reins and jerked his weary horse awake. "Tell your people when I come to be ready for me. Tell them to put out all their fires. Fire is the only thing in the whole world that I'm afraid of. It's the only thing in God's world that can destroy me."

Saynday watched Smallpox and his death horse traveling north, away from the Kiowas. Then he took out his flint and steel, and set fire to the spindly prairie grass at his feet. The winds came and picked up the fire, and carried it to make a ring of safety around the Kiowas' camps.

"Perhaps I can still be some good to my people after all," Saynday said to himself, feeling better.

And that's the way it was, and that's the way it is, to this good day.

▼▼▼▼▼

Told to Alice Marriott by Frank Givens (Eagle Plume).

Tsali of the Cherokees

From the mist-world of folk history, we move into the world of written history, and of events that have been recorded as well as told.

The legend of Tsali is well known and well documented in the non-Indian sense, but it is still part of Cherokee oral tradition, as well. Tsali and his family were real persons, living in a real place. But in a sense their story is the story of all the Cherokees of the early nineteenth century, and, as it is told here, is recorded from the word-of-mouth telling of one of Tsali's descendants.

This is the way that legends are made. The true story of a real person becomes a symbol for the history of his people. So George Washington stands for the courage and virtue of the Revolutionaries, Benjamin Franklin for their astuteness and diplomacy, and Thomas Jefferson for their farseeing wisdom. In the same way, Tsali stands as a symbol of the courage, loyalty, and devotion of all the Cherokees.

In the time when their troubles began, the ordinary Cherokees did not at first understand that anything was really wrong. They knew that their tribal chiefs traveled back and forth to the white man's place called Washington more often than they used to do. They knew that when the chiefs came back from that place there were quarrels in the tribal council.

Up in the hills and the back country, where the *Ani Keetoowah* —the true Cherokees—lived, word of the changes came more slowly than the changes themselves came to the valley Cherokees. Many of the hill people never left their farm lands, and those who did went only to the nearest trading post and back. Few travelers ever came into the uplands, where the mists of the Smokies shut out the encroaching world.

So, when the news came that some of the chiefs of the Cherokees had touched the pen, and put their names or their marks on a paper, and agreed by doing so that this was no longer Cherokee country, the *Ani Keetoowah* could not believe what they heard. Surely, they said to each other, this news must be false. No Cherokee—not even a mixed-blood—would sign away his own and his people's lands. But that was what the chiefs had done.

Then the word came that the chiefs were even more divided among themselves, and that not all of them had touched the pen. Some were not willing to move away to the new lands across the Mississippi, and settle in the hills around Fort Gibson, Oklahoma.

"Perhaps we should hang on," the *Ani Keetoowah* said to one another. "Perhaps we will not have to go away after all." They waited and hoped, although they knew in their hearts that hope is the cruelest curse on mankind.

One of the leaders of the *Ani Keetoowah* was Tsali. The white men had trouble pronouncing his name, so they called him "Charley," or "Dutch." Tsali was a full-blood, and so were his wife and their family. They were of the oldest *Keetoowah* Cherokee blood, and would never have let themselves be shamed by having half-breed relatives.

Tsali and his four sons worked two hillsides and the valley between them, in the southern part of the hill country. Tsali and his wife and their youngest son lived in a log house at the head of the hollow. The others had their own homes, spread out along the hillsides. They grew corn and beans, a few English peas, squashes and pumpkins, tobacco and cotton, and even a little sugar cane and indigo. Tsali's wife kept chickens in a fenced run away from the house.

The women gathered wild hemp and spun it; they spun the cotton, and the wool from their sheep. Then they wove the thread into cloth, and sometimes in winter when their few cattle and the sheep had been cared for and the chickens fed and there was not much else to do, the men helped at the looms which they had built themselves. The women did all the cutting and the making of garments for the whole family.

Tsali and his family were not worldly rich, in the way that the chiefs and some of the Cherokees of the valley towns were rich. They had hardly seen white man's metal money in their lives. But Tsali's people never lacked for food, or good clothing, or safe shelter.

The missionaries seldom came into the uplands then. Tsali took his sons and their wives, and his own wife, to the great dance ground where the seven *Keetoowah* villages gathered each month at the time of the full moon. There they danced their prayers in time to the beating of the women's terrapin-shell leg rattles, around and around the mound of packed white ashes on top of which bloomed the eternal fire that was the life of all the Cherokees.

The occasional missionaries fussed over the children. They gave them white men's names, so that by Tsali's time everyone had an Indian name and an English one. The Cherokees listened to the missionaries politely, for the missionaries were great gossips, and the Cherokees heard their news and ignored the rest of their words.

"You will have to go soon," said one white preacher to Tsali. "There's no hope this time. The lands have all been sold and the Georgia troopers are moving in. You'll have to go west."

"We'll never leave," Tsali answered. "This is our land and we belong to it. Who could take it from us—who would want it? It's hard even for us to farm here, and we're used to hill farming. The white men wouldn't want to come here—they'll want the rich lands in the valleys, if the lowland people will give them up."

"They want these hills more than any other land," the missionary said. He sounded almost threatening. "Don't you see, you poor ignorant Indian? They are finding gold—gold, man, gold—downstream in the lower *Keetoowah* country. That means that the source of the gold is in the headwaters of the rivers that flow from here down into the valleys. I've seen gold dust in those streams myself."

"Gold?" asked Tsali. "You mean this yellow stuff?" And he took a buckskin pouch out of the pouch that hung from his sash, and opened it. At the sight of the yellow dust the pouch contained, the missionary seemed to go a little crazy.

"That's it!" he cried. "Where did you get it? How did you find it? You'll be rich if you can get more."

"We find it in the rivers, as you said," Tsali replied. "We gather what we need to take to the trader. I have this now because I am going down to the valley in a few days, to get my wife some ribbons to trim her new dress."

"Show me where you got it," the missionary begged. "We can all be rich. I'll protect you from the other white men, if you make me your partner."

"No, I think I'd better not," said Tsali thoughtfully. "My sons are my partners, as I was my father's. We do not need another partner, and, as long as we have our old squirrel guns, we do not need to be protected. Thank you, but you can go on. We are better off as we are."

The missionary coaxed and threatened, but Tsali stood firm. In the end, the white man went away, without any gold except a pinch that Tsali gave him, because the missionary seemed to value the yellow dust even more than the trader did.

Then it was time to go to the trading post. When Tsali came in the store, the trader said to him, "Well, Chief, glad to see you. I hear you're a rich man these days."

"I have always been a rich man," Tsali answered. "I have my family and we all have our good health. We have land to farm, houses to live in, food on our tables, and enough clothes. Most of all, we have the love in our hearts for each other and our friends. Indeed, you are right. We are very rich."

"That's one way of looking at it," said the trader, "but it isn't what I was thinking about. From what I hear, there's gold on your land. You've got a gold mine."

"A gold man?" repeated Tsali. "I never heard of a gold man."

"No!" shouted the trader. "A gold *mine*, I said. A place where you can go and pick up gold."

"Oh, that!" Tsali exclaimed. "Yes, we have some places like that on our land. Here's some of the yellow dust we find there."

And he opened the pouch to show the trader. The trader had seen pinches of Tsali's gold dust before, and taken it in trade, without saying much about it. Now he went as crazy as the missionary. "Don't tell anybody else about this, Charley," he whispered, leaning over the counter. "We'll just keep it to ourselves. I'll help you work it out, and I'll keep the other white men away. We'll all be rich."

"Thank you," said Tsali, "but I don't believe I want to be rich that way. I just want enough of this stuff to trade you for ribbons and sugar."

"Oh, all right," answered the trader sulkily, "have it your own way. But don't blame me if you're sorry afterwards."

"I won't blame anybody," said Tsali, and bought his ribbon.

A month later, when the Georgia militia came riding up the valley to Tsali's house, the missionary and the trader were with them. The men all stopped in front of the house, and Tsali's wife came out into the dog-trot, the open-ended passage that divided the two halves of the house and made a cool breezeway where the family sat in warm weather. She spoke to the men.

"Won't you come in and sit down?"

"Where's the old man?" the militia captain asked.

"Why, he's working out in the fields," said Amanda. "Sit down and have a cool drink of water while I send the boy for him."

"Send the boy quickly," the captain ordered. "We'll wait in our saddles and not trouble to get down."

"All right, if you'd rather not," Amanda said. "Do you mind telling me why you're here?"

"We're here to put you off this place," said the captain. "Haven't you heard? This isn't Cherokee land any more; the chiefs signed it over to the government, and now it's open for settlement. One or the other of these two gentlemen will probably claim it."

"They can't do that!" Amanda protested. "It's our land—nobody else's. The chiefs had no right to sign it away. My husband's father worked this place, and his father before him. This is our home. This is where we belong."

"No more," said the captain. "You belong in the removal camps down by the river, with the rest of the Indians. They're going to start shipping the Cherokees west tomorrow morning."

Amanda sat down on the bench in the dog-trot, with her legs trembling under her. "All of us?" she asked.

"Every one of you."

"Let me call my son and send him for his daddy," Amanda said.

"Hurry up!"

Amanda went into the house, calling to the boy, who was just fourteen and had been standing, listening, behind the door. She gave him his father's old squirrel gun, and he sneaked his own blow-gun and darts and slid out the back of the house. Amanda went back to the dog-trot and sat and waited. She sat there and waited, while the missionary, the trader, and the captain quarreled about which of their wives should cook in her kitchen. She let them quarrel, and hoped her men were all right.

Tsali and his older sons were working the overhill corn field, when the boy came panting up, and told them what had happened.

"Is your mother all right?" Tsali asked.

"She was when I left," the boy answered.

"We'll hide in the woods till they're gone," Tsali told his older sons. "If they find us, they'll have to kill us to put us off this land."

"What about the women?" the oldest son asked.

"They'll be all right," Tsali answered. "Your mother's a quick-thinking woman; she'll take care of them. If we can hide in the caves by the river till dark, we'll go back then and get them."

They slipped away into the woods, downhill to the river, taking the boy with them, although he offered to go back and tell the white men he couldn't find his father.

All afternoon Amanda waited. Her daughters-in-law saw the strange men and horses in front of the big house, and came to join her. At dusk, the captain gave up and ordered his men to make camp in the front yard. "We'll wait here until the men come back," he said.

With the white men camped all around the house, the women went into the kitchen and barred all the doors. It was a long time before the campfires made from the fence pickets ceased to blaze and began to smolder. It was a longer time until the women heard it—a scratch on the back door, so soft and so light that it would have embarrassed a mouse. Amanda slid back the bar, and Tsali and his sons slipped into the darkened room. There was just enough moonlight for them to make out each other's shapes.

"We came to get you," Tsali said. "Come quickly. Leave everything except your knives. Don't wait a minute."

Amanda and her daughters-in-law always wore their knives at their belts, so they were ready. One at a time, Tsali last, the whole family crept out of their home and escaped into the woods.

In the morning, when the white men stretched and scratched and woke, the *Ani Keetoowah* were gone.

It was spring, and the weather was warm, but the rain fell and soaked the Cherokees. They had brought no food, and they dared not fire a gun. One of the daughters-in-law was pregnant, and her time was close. Amanda was stiff and crippled with rheumatism. They gathered wild greens, for it was too early for berries or plums, and the men and boy trapped small animals and birds in string snares the women made by pulling out their hair and twisting it.

Day by day, for four weeks, the starving family listened to white men beating through the woods. The Cherokees were tired and cold and hungry, but they were silent. They even began to hope that in time the white men would go away, and the Indians would be safe.

It was not to be. One trooper brought his dog, and the dog caught the human scent. So the dog, with his man behind him, came sniffing into the cave and Tsali and his family were caught before the men could pick up their loaded guns.

The militiaman shouted, and other white men came thudding through the woods. They tied the Cherokee men's hands behind them, and bound them all together along a rope. The militiamen pushed Tsali and his sons through the woods. The women followed, weeping.

At last they were back at their own house, but they would not have recognized it. The troopers had plundered the garden, and trampled the plants they didn't eat. The door from the kitchen into the dog-trot hung askew, and the door to the main room had been wrenched off its hinges. Clothes and bedding lay in filthy piles around the yard. What the militiamen could not use, they ruined.

"Oh, my garden!" cried Amanda, and, when she saw the scattered feathers, "Oh, my little hens!"

"What are you going to do with us?" Tsali demanded.

"Take you down to the river. The last boat is loading today. There's still time to get you on it and out of here."

"I—will—not—go," Tsali said quietly. "You—nor you—nor you—nobody can make me go."

"Our orders are to take all the Cherokees. If any resist, shoot them."

"Shoot me, then!" cried Tsali. The captain raised his rifle.

"Stop!" Amanda screamed. She stepped over beside her husband. "If you shoot, shoot us both," she ordered. "Our lives have been one life since we were no older than our boy here. I don't want to go on living without my husband. And I cannot leave our home any more than he can. Shoot us both."

The four sons stepped forward. "We will die with our parents," the oldest one said. "Take our wives to the boat, if that is the only place where they can be safe, but we stay here." He turned to his wife and the other young women.

"That is my order as your husband," Tsali's son said. "You must go away to the west, and make new lives for yourselves while you are still young enough to do so." The wives sobbed, and held out their arms, but the husbands turned their backs on the women. "We will stay with our parents," all the young men said.

The young boy, too, stood with his brothers, beside his father. "Let this boy go," Tsali said to the white men. "He is so young. A man grows, and plants his seed, and his seed goes on. This is my seed. I planted it. My older sons and I have had our chances. They will leave children, and their names will never be forgotten. But this boy is too young. His seed has not ripened for planting yet. Let him go, to care for his sisters, on the way to the west."

"Very well," said the captain. "He can't do much harm if he

does live." He turned to two militiamen. "Take the boy and the young women away," he ordered. "Keep them going till they come to the boats, and load them on board."

The young women and the boy, stunned and silenced, were driven down the road before they could say good-by, nor would the troopers let them look back. Behind them, as they started on the long main road, they heard the sound of the shots.

▼▼▼▼▼▼

Told to Alice Marriott by Norah Roper, granddaughter of Tsali and Sequoyah.

Yellow Hair:
George Armstrong Custer

▼▼▼▼▼▼▼▼▼▼▼▼▼▼▼ C H E Y E N N E AND A R A P A H O

That strange and ambiguous personality, George Armstrong Custer, has left his mark on American history and legend in many ways. Brevet Major General during the Civil War, his rank was reduced to that of Lieutenant Colonel in the regular Army after hostilities ceased. One can distinguish Custer aficionados pro and con by which title they use in referring to him.

No one will ever know for certain what happened on that sunny July morning in 1876 when battle tore up and down the slopes of the hill beside the Little Big Horn. The white men who knew what orders had been given Custer and the other officers of the Seventh Cavalry, and whether those orders were obeyed or disobeyed, never committed themselves, for Custer's widow was alive and until her adoring eyes closed they remained officers and gentlemen—and silent. And Elizabeth Bacon Custer outlived them all. We only know that the battle of the Little Big Horn was a true battle in every sense of the word, fought by seasoned troops under trained commanders on both sides.

This one battle marked the greatest, and almost the only, confederation of Plains Indian tribes in their history. Sioux, Cheyenne, and

155

*Arapaho joined forces in a last desperate struggle to drive the whites
out of the plains if possible; if that could not be done, out of the
sacred land of the Black Hills of the Dakotas and of the Devil's
Tower, Wyoming. Momentarily they succeeded, but in the end it was a
costly victory, ending in the ghastly tragicomedy of Sitting Bull in
Buffalo Bill's Wild West Show, bowing over Queen Victoria's hand.*

▼▼▼▼▼▼

After the treaty of Medicine Lodge Creek, in 1871, the Cheyennes and
the Arapahos, who were old allies, sat in the council tipi together. All
the leading chiefs were unhappy and disturbed, for among the white
men present at the signing of the treaty had been Yellow Hair—
George Armstrong Custer.

Custer was known to have a Cheyenne wife and a half-Cheyenne
son. The same man who disobeyed his commanding officer's orders so
that he might make a dash to Fort Riley, Kansas, to see his white wife,
also spent many nights in a Cheyenne tipi. How could the chiefs trust
him? He would trick women, disavow his son's parentage, and lie to
his friends. He could not be trusted.

They sent a young man, as messenger, with a word that Custer
should come to Black Kettle's camp and smoke with him. Black Kettle
was a peace chief of the Cheyennes—an old man, loved and respected
by everybody. His wife prepared a feast for the visitors and they all
sat down and ate together.

After the feast, the young messenger brought Black Kettle a pipe
bag. It was of the finest fawn skin, and was beaded in horizontal red,
yellow, black, and white bands. Black Kettle's wife belonged to the
women's secret society, and she had the right to make that kind of
beadwork.

From the bag, Black Kettle drew out a T-shaped pipe of red pipe-
stone, with a straight white dogwood stem. He fitted the stem to the
pipe bowl, and filled the pipe with native tobacco mixed with shredded
sumac bark. Very carefully Black Kettle lifted a coal from the tipi
fire, using a pair of sticks for tongs, and lighted the pipe. When he
had blown smoke to Maheo above, to mother the Earth, and to the four
corners of the world, Black Kettle spoke.

"Yellow Hair," he said, "we have called you to our council because we all wish to make a peace and keep the peace. We have set our
marks on paper, but that is the white man's way. Now we ask you to
swear the peace in the Indian way, too. Smoke with us, Yellow
Hair."

Custer tossed back the long yellow locks that lay on the shoulders of his fringed and beaded buckskin shirt. He never wore a uniform if he could help it and that was another thing the Indians didn't like. If he joined the soldiers, if he gave orders to the soldiers, then he should dress like them. The yellow locks might be thinning on top, but they still hung thick from the sides and back, and fell across his shoulders.

One thing every Indian knew about Custer, he never smoked. Even smelling tobacco smoke, he said, made him feel sick. But success and advancement depended on his control of these Indians, so Yellow Hair put out his hand for the pipe.

Yellow Hair followed Black Kettle's motions, and let a little smoke trickle from his mouth to each of the six directions. He didn't swallow any smoke, but he put the pipe to his mouth six times, and blew out six puffs of tobacco smoke. Now Custer was joined to the Cheyennes and the Arapahos in what the Indians hoped would be a lasting and safe peace. The other chiefs smoked in their turns.

"Now, Yellow Hair," Black Kettle said, "you have smoked with us, and promised us peace. You may go."

Custer left the tipi, denting the ground with the heels of his boots. Black Kettle shook the dottle from the pipe into the palm of his hand, and sprinkled a pinch of it in every heel print.

"Yellow Hair has gone," he said. "Hear me, my chiefs. If he breaks the promise he has made us today, he will die, and he will die a coward's death. No Indian will soil his hands with Yellow Hair's scalp."

"Hah-ho," said all the other chiefs. "So be it. If Yellow Hair breaks the promise he has sworn in the peace treaty, then let him die a woman's death."

Two years later Black Kettle and his band made their winter camp on the banks of the Washita River. It was a peace camp, a settled camp. There were brush windbreaks around many of the tipis, and the children played in safety. In the center of the camp stood the beautifully beaded tipi where Black Kettle and his wife lived, and to one side of them and to the other were the keepers of the Cheyenne sacred medicines.

The weather was bitterly cold, for a blue norther had swept across the plains that afternoon, and everyone shivered under its weight of hail and sleet. People huddled inside their tipis, away from the force of the wind; sat close to their fires, and, after they had eaten dinner, told stories of the old days and the old ways. It was a rich camp. The women of Black Kettle's band worked hard, and they were well supplied with dried meat, fine clothes, and painted, beaded, and quill-embroidered robes.

By midnight the camp was silent, and then Yellow Hair struck. He and his troopers, with the storm at their backs, had ridden the seventy miles from Camp Supply in two days, and now, in the darkness, they attacked the peace camp.

Custer had divided his forces, sending a small detachment of troopers downstream to attack a camp of visiting Arapahos. He, with the main body of troops, struck at Black Kettle's camp. The old man died in the ruins of his flaming tipi and fell with the United States flag—given him at Medicine Lodge as a token of the peace he was to keep—still clutched in his hand. Black Kettle's wife stabbed herself and fell dead across her husband's body.

Downstream there was shooting at the Arapaho camp, and then there was no more shooting.

The troops of the Seventh Cavalry gathered together all the wealth of Black Kettle's camp and set fire to every beautiful thing those Cheyennes possessed. Even some of the soldiers cried when they saw the destruction of robes and food belonging to women and children.

By daylight, with Sharp's carbines, the troopers shot all the horses in the great herds pastured across the river.

And still there was no more shooting from downstream. Yellow Hair sent a detachment to see if the Arapahos had been wiped out like the Cheyennes. The troops found that the Arapahos and their camp were gone. On the ground were the bodies of Major Joel Eliot and his men—all scalped.

Yellow Hair had broken the peace, but his men had died like men.

Now the proud Cheyennes became for a time a broken people. They suffered imprisonment, and death from disease and starvation. Yellow Hair reported his great victory over Black Kettle, but he also had to report that he had let men be killed without sending them support. Even "Woosinton" could not let that go by. They sent for Yellow Hair to go east, and they punished him by making him stay there for one whole year.

Then Yellow Hair and his white wife came back to Fort Abraham Lincoln. His Cheyenne wife had died of grief, and her sisters had taken her son and hidden him, so he could be raised as an Indian. Fort Abraham Lincoln was far away, north on the Yellowstone, so the southern Cheyennes sat and waited and worked out a plan.

Quietly, messengers moved from tribe to tribe, up and down the plains. They went to the Arapahos, of course, and to the many different bands of Sioux. The Crows and the Pawnees, who had taken the white man's uniforms, and served the Army as scouts, the messengers avoided.

In time, just as quietly, the villages moved. A few camps at a time drifted into the territory of Sitting Bull, the Hunkpapa Sioux chief. Here the groups spread out, along the Little Big Horn and Tongue rivers, and waited until all the men were armed and ready.

The Crows and Pawnees came into Fort Abraham Lincoln with word that the tribes were gathering. They might attack the white settlements or the fort. Trouble was on its way.

There was a council of the white soldiers, and General Terry, the commanding officer at the post, gave his orders. Yellow Hair would go one way, he himself would go another, and Major Marcus Reno would go the third. They would all come together to surround the great camp on the Little Big Horn.

With Custer would ride his brother, Lieutenant Tom Custer, and Captain Myles W. Keogh. Captain Keogh was famous everywhere for his devotion to his big bay gelding, Comanche. The two talked to each other like brothers, and Comanche seemed to know what the Captain thought before the words had formed in the man's mind.

The night before they set out, these three men, with some other officers, gathered in Custer's quarters for a farewell dinner. Elizabeth Custer and her Negro cook, Eliza, provided a good one, of venison, and roast sage hens, and any other game the men had brought in. Late in the evening, Tom Custer, Yellow Hair, and Keogh shaved their heads with horse clippers. Elizabeth wept when she saw the fading golden locks fall to the floor; then she comforted herself with the thought that perhaps the Indians would be less likely to recognize and attack her husband if they did not see his long hair.

Early in the morning, the troops rode out of the fort, and the women watched them go. Some women wept, and others held back their tears and bravely waved their handkerchiefs in good-by. As the women and the post guard watched and the band played "The Girl I Left Behind Me" and the regimental marching song, "Garry Owen," one of those miracles of plains light appeared. Riding above the troopers were their images, mirrored against the sky by a mirage. Someone cried, "They are riding to their death!" but the shout was quickly stilled.

If the Pawnees and the Crows knew what was happening in the Indian camps, the Sioux, the Cheyenne, and the Arapaho knew what was happening at Fort Abraham Lincoln. They were prepared, and when the charge came the Indians met it like rocks.

Custer and his troops were driven back, and took refuge on top of a steep hill, almost a bluff, north of the Little Big Horn. There the Indians could surround them, and slowly, methodically, tear them to pieces. Major Reno was pinned downstream by the Arapahos. General

Terry had not yet come up in support. Yellow Hair died as Major Eliot had died, in the center of a ring of soldiers, killed by ''the finest light cavalry in the world.''

The Indian women struck camp and loaded their horses while the battle still went on. When victory came, the Indians melted away into the Black Hills. By the time General Terry relieved Major Reno, and rescued his detachment, the only being left alive on the hilltop was Captain Keogh's great horse, Comanche. The dead man's hand still clutched the reins. Those two were like brothers and no Indian would separate them. Later, General Terry took Comanche to Fort Riley, Kansas, and there he lived until he died of old age—no rider ever mounted him again, but he was led in every review on the post. Comanche's body is still preserved in the Kansas State Historical Museum.

Whether, as the Cheyennes say, no one recognized Yellow Hair with his head shaved; whether, as the Arapahos say, he was a coward and not worth scalping, we do not know. We do know that his body, unlike others on that battlefield, was not mutilated. Yellow Hair lay on his back, with a woman's knife thrust through his chest, but he was dead before that Cheyenne woman struck him, so they say.

▼▼▼▼▼

Told to Alice Marriott and Carol K. Rachlin by Mary Little Bear Inkanish and John Stands-in-the-Timber, and John Fletcher, Cheyennes, and by Richard Pratt, Arapaho.

The Deer Woman

The Siouan-speaking Ponca, with their affiliates, the Osage, Omaha, Oto, and Quapah, were among the tribes who lived between the Mississippi and the true High Plains. Their cultures shared traits from both east and west; horticulture was combined with hunting; mat houses were clustered in permanent villages, but tipis were carried on the communal hunts. They both plaited fabrics and painted hides.

In the story that follows we have another legend. Most Poncas—as well as members of other tribes—still believe that the Deer Woman exists, and that she is the head of a prostitution ring. Oral tradition has it that until the Deer Woman is captured and destroyed no Indian woman will be really safe away from her family. In this legend we have an example of the survival into contemporary society of an ancient belief in witchcraft and the power of evil.

▼▼▼▼▼▼

A long time ago, when the Poncas used to live in Nebraska, before they were moved to Oklahoma, young men sometimes saw the Deer Woman.

Everyone in the village would be dancing and happy. Perhaps they were celebrating a victory, and the girls carried scalps on poles to

161

show how brave their brothers were, and how many enemies their brothers had touched and killed. The old men would build a big fire, and the young women would dance sidewise, in a ring, around it. Sometimes they joined hands, and the dancing ring was linked. The young men danced alone, between the circling wall of women and the fire, leaping and prancing.

The woman came from nowhere, and nobody knew her. Suddenly she slipped into the line between two girls, holding each of them by the hand. She was very beautiful. Her hair streamed like black water over her white buckskin dress. If the other dancers had looked at the woman's feet, they would have seen that she had a deer's hooves, over which no moccasins would fit. But nobody ever looked anywhere but at her eyes. No matter how rude a person felt, to stare so at another, he could not help looking into those magic deep black eyes. Besides, everybody was busy dancing and being happy. They didn't think about looking down; all their thoughts and their looks were upward.

As the night grew later, one young man would find a girl, and then another young girl would find a man. A couple at a time, they slipped away from the dancing ring into the bushes, and there they spent the night.

While she danced, the Deer Woman looked at the young men and chose her partner, but only for the night. Whoever she chose was helpless. He could not go to any other woman, no matter how much he loved and wanted her. The Deer Woman held him with her magic eyes, and when the moon was lowest but the night not yet dark, she drew him away beside her, into the brush.

In the morning, someone found the young man. He lay dead, on his back, his body stripped and naked to the daylight. Anyone who saw him knew how he had died, for when the Deer Woman had taken her pleasure from him, she beat and trampled his genitals with her knife-edge hooves. Even if he had lived, he would never have been a man again.

And that was long ago, when the Poncas still lived in Nebraska. They lived in mat houses, they cooked their meat in earthen pots, and they carved their weapons from stone and wood. The Deer Woman came and went among them, and they could do nothing to stop her.

Nowadays, the Poncas live in Oklahoma. Some of them are rich, with oil wells or coal mines on their lands. They get good lease money from their allotments, those rich Poncas.

Other Poncas today are poverty-poor. In winter, if they cannot get on the relief rolls, they suffer. Sometimes even the children must live on tight belts and water, and their parents have only the tight belts.

Rich or poor, however, the Poncas still dance. Every Labor Day weekend, they gather in the woods south of Ponca City, and there they hold their powwow. They have fine camp grounds, with shade, and plenty of firewood, and good water. Other tribes come to visit the Poncas at that time.

The Poncas camp in the grove, setting their tents in the same relative positions that their ancestors' houses stood in the old villages. But the visitors cluster their camps on high ground, in the sparsest shade, away from the wells, the ration distribution, and the dance ring. They would rather walk a long way for everything than risk getting too near the Deer Woman.

The Ponca dance ring is not like any other. Instead of being out in the open, it has solid concrete walls, seven feet high, with bleachers built against them. Any Indians who wish may come into the ring free, but people who are not Indians are charged admission to sit in the concrete bleachers and watch the dancing. That is the custom of the Poncas. The other tribes never charge to watch the dancing. The Poncas have their own ways, different from other people's.

Inside the dance ring, as always, the circling wall of women surrounds the clustered drummers and the leaping young men. In the round dances that open and close the evening, the young men join the women, and they all circle around the drummers. When the men are war-dancing freely in the center of the ring, the women dance in groups, spokes of friends stepping and stretching out from the hub that is the drum. Three or four women dance together, bending forward or from side to side as the drum tells them to, straightening and moving forward spoke-wise when the beat changes.

Some time in the evening a strange woman appears. She dances alone around the drum. No friends join her. She wears a beautiful white shawl, and her hair streams over her shoulders. Her eyes are deep and black, and hold another's so tightly that he cannot look at her feet. Anyone who dances behind her where those eyes cannot reach him, and who happens to look down, will see that her feet are not a woman's feet, but the hooves of a deer.

No one knows who the woman is or where she comes from. No one knows how or where she lives when she is not dancing. For late at night, when the stomp-dance lines circle and twist about the fire, the Deer Woman disappears. Nowadays, instead of a young man, she takes a young woman with her.

Sometimes the girl is found the next morning, lying in the woods, beaten and bloody. She has never been sexually assaulted, but she may be crippled for life. When those girls recover consciousness, they cannot clearly remember what happened to them. They all say they got into a car with an older woman, and were driven away from the dance grounds. After that, they remember nothing.

Sometimes the girls disappear, and are not seen again until long afterward. Then it may be that a man who has come to the city without his wife will find one of them walking beside him, suddenly, on the street, late at night. When she speaks to him, the man must join the girl, go with her to her furnished room, and later pay her well. A few girls have come home to have babies, but when their babies are weaned, the girls give the babies to their grandparents to be reared, and return to the city. The Deer Woman has those girls and she holds them well.

The men at Ponca dances have waited and watched for the Deer Woman, in order to protect the girls from her. Some fathers and brothers who have lost daughters or sisters say that they are willing to kill the Deer Woman to protect the other women of their families from her.

No one has ever caught the Deer Woman. She comes to the Ponca powwow every other year. Once the men were watching for her. They kept their eyes on the ground, and would not look up at any woman's face. The men were not fixed by the Deer Woman's eyes, so this time they saw her feet. One sprang at her and almost caught her in his arms, but the Deer Woman jumped that seven-foot wall around the dance ring and was gone.

Someday, say the Ponca men. Someday they will catch up with the Deer Woman.

▼▼▼▼▼

Told to Alice Marriott and Carol K. Rachlin by informants from several tribes who prefer their names withheld.

The Dancing Feather

As the story of the Deer Woman makes clear, the contemporary powwow, at which members of many tribes gather to camp, visit, exchange information, and dance, is a great binding force, tribally and intertribally. The term "Pan-Indian" has been coined by anthropologists to describe the exchange of customs that goes on at a powwow.

Nevertheless, whatever the interchange of ideas, tribal identity remains strong. Pawnees do not camp near Kiowas, nor Apaches near Poncas. Each tribe has its own way of dressing and dancing, its own style of drumming, and its own camping customs and traditions, and maintains them.

A few years ago the war-dance contest was held at the Tulsa Powwow. It was late in the summer, and terribly hot. During the day the people sat in the shade in the camps and played squaw dice. It was too hot for races, or for archery matches, or even for giveaways. The people gave their presents to their friends in the evenings. Naturally, that made the evening dancing slower than usual, because it takes a long time to make the speeches and presentations that go with ceremonial gifts. It was almost midnight when they got to the war-dance contests.

Every night of the preliminary contests, Jimmy Bob was ahead. He was a Cheyenne, and a fine dancer. People had admired him for a long time, but they had never seen him dance as well as he did that year.

Dewey Legrange, an Oto, was right behind Jimmy Bob. It was a dead heat between them every night of the preliminaries, and sometimes the judges had a hard time deciding which man had the finest timing and the best footwork. They were even right up to the last night.

In the morning, Jimmy Bob's mother got up early to go for water. Jimmy would have been willing to go, and his mother knew it, but she wanted him to sleep so he would be fresh for the dancing that night. Her husband was a drummer, and she wanted him to be fresh, too, because she knew it would encourage their boy to do his best if he saw his father drumming and singing for him.

The well was clear on the other side of the camp, and Jimmy's mother decided to take one bucket at a time; two would be heavy to carry for about a quarter of a mile. It was a bright clear morning, with the red sun just inching over the horizon, and the grass was dry under her feet. Jimmy's mother noticed those two things, and she thought that perhaps together they meant that rain would come. She hoped the rain would hold off until after the dance contest, because wet moccasins burn a dancer's feet and slow him down.

As Jimmy's mother—Carrie, her name was—came near the well, she thought she saw the flutter of a woman's skirt moving away from it. Carrie paid no attention to the woman; it might be a girl who had been out all night, going home to her parents' camp; it might be a married woman who had slipped out; it might be a housewife like herself, who had come early for water.

Carrie filled her bucket and started back to her own tent. As she went, she passed an Oto camp. An old woman, Dewey's grandmother, was sitting up on her bed, combing her long hair, but everyone else was sleeping. Carrie called, "Good morning," softly, so as not to wake anyone else, but the old woman paid no attention to her. She just went on combing her hair.

When Carrie came back with her second bucket, and filled it at the well, she noticed that the water was not as clear as it had been before. It was riled and muddy, and little sticks and pieces of grass were floating around in it.

Well, that happens, Carrie thought to herself. Some people are careless when they draw water. They don't think about others, who will come after them. It will settle by the time I need it to wash the dishes. And she filled the second bucket and went back to her own camp.

The men slept until way up in the morning—almost seven o'clock. Carrie had a cup of coffee and some fried bread and bacon and eggs ready for them, and they all ate breakfast together. After the meal, Jimmy Bob went over to the water buckets, and took a long drink from the dipper. It wasn't until afterward that his mother noticed that he drank from the second bucket—the one with the muddy water in it. But when she went to look, the water had settled and cleared, and was all right.

The last day of any powwow is a nice day, and this was no exception. Friends who could only get away for the one day kept coming in, and Carrie had her hands full feeding them and cleaning up after the meals. Her husband and son talked to the guests and entertained them. About three o'clock everyone but the family left for the squaw dice game, and they were alone in camp.

"You know," Jimmy Bob said, "I don't know what's the matter with me. I seem to have a catch in my leg."

"You can't do that," said Harry, his father. "You have to win that contest tonight. The prize is a hundred dollars."

"I know it is," answered Jimmy Bob. "Think I'd forget it? I'm counting on that money to pay my tuition at the university."

"Which leg is it?" Carrie asked.

"The right one."

"Let me see it," Harry said. "Maybe I can rub the pain out like with a horse." Harry always was a great one to manage horses.

Jimmy Bob stretched out on his bed, face down, and his father took his right leg in his hand, and started to rub.

"There seems to be a lump in your calf, like a charley horse," Harry observed. He worked and rubbed the leg for about an hour, and Jimmy Bob said he felt better and the pain had gone.

"I can dance all right tonight," he reassured his parents.

Carrie and Harry went to the dance ring early, leaving Jimmy Bob at home dressing. His father had already painted Jimmy's face, and they knew that if they stayed around the tent to help their boy get dressed they would only make him nervous.

The group dancing and the giveaways dragged along, as they had every other night, as if there would never be a war-dance contest. At last, though, everyone was satisfied, the last round dance was over, and the contest could begin.

Carrie sat on her bench and watched. Jimmy Bob had danced just enough that evening to get limbered up and in good shape, not enough to tire him. His mother thought he was dancing better than ever, and that Dewey Legrange didn't have a chance.

"Come on, you boys," called the master of ceremonies. "We'll have a short slow war dance first, for a warm up. You drummers, take over."

The boys were as equal as they ever were, Carrie thought as she watched them. Dewey was a good dancer, all right. And then she noticed something. Her boy was slowing down. He was still on the beat with the drum, but his legs seemed to hang heavily in the air. She glanced across at Harry, and saw by the anxious look in his face that he had noticed the same thing.

"Now the fast war dance!" the master of ceremonies cried, and the drum speeded up and the dancers with it. Then all at once Jimmy Bob froze, there in the center of the dance ring, his right leg sticking straight out in front of him in the air. And he hadn't stopped on the beat, either.

The judges ran up, and talked to him, and felt his leg. Harry came over and began to rub. But the dance contest was over, and Dewey Legrange had won.

Jimmy Bob's parents helped him back to camp, and laid him on his cot. Harry helped him out of his dance costume. His father rubbed and rubbed, and finally Jimmy Bob could get his leg down, flat on the cot, but that was about all he could do. He could sit up, but he couldn't walk.

The next morning Harry and Carrie helped Jimmy Bob lie down in the back of their station wagon, and drove him to the Public Health Service hospital. The doctors examined him, and found the lump in his calf muscles, but they couldn't find any reason for it. The doctors took X-rays and used fluoroscopes, and did everything they knew how to do, but they couldn't find a broken bone or a strained muscle or anything. All the poking and prodding hurt so much that Jimmy Bob was about to cry, and Carrie really did.

"Take him on home," the doctor finally said. "He can soak the leg in a hot bath and maybe the muscles will loosen up." He gave Jimmy Bob a shot of penicillin and a bottle of aspirin for good measure, and the family went home.

For four days they tried soaking the leg in hot water. Jimmy Bob took the aspirin. Nothing helped, and at last they took him to the emergency room at the local hospital. Things were no better there. Nobody could find out what was wrong.

"These boys will go on dancing till they wear themselves out," the intern said. He looked young enough to go dancing himself. "We'll just have to wait and see." But he gave Jimmy Bob another shot of penicillin and some more aspirin before they left, all the same.

The family waited another four days. Then Harry got up in the morning and set his mouth like an old army mule.

"White man's medicine isn't any good for these things," he said. "I dreamed last night. Somebody shot poison into my boy, and that's what happened. We'll take him to an Indian doctor."

There was a famous Indian doctor in town not far away. The parents put their son into the back of the station wagon and started out. But first they bought four things: a watermelon, four yards of white cloth, Bull Durham tobacco, and a sack of dried corn. They knew the doctor would want an eagle feather, too, but there was a law against buying and selling eagle feathers, so Harry pulled one out of his fan.

When they got to the Indian doctor's house, the old man seemed to be expecting them. "Get down," he said. Harry and Carrie helped Jimmy Bob into the house and laid him on the floor, where the old man showed them to place him.

"Now I'll X-ray him," said the Indian doctor, and he took out an old black silk handkerchief, and laid it over Jimmy Bob's leg. "I need an eagle feather," the doctor went on, and Harry handed him one without speaking.

The doctor shaded his eyes with the eagle feather and peered at the black silk.

"There it is! I see it!" the doctor said, when he had looked thoroughly. He took the eagle feather, and began to brush with it, gathering all the evil that had settled on Jimmy Bob into a pile in the middle of his calf.

Then the Indian doctor got out a hollowed-out tip of a cow's horn. He took a stone knife-blade, and cut crisscross scratches over the pile of invisible evil. He put the cow's horn over the cuts, and began to suck. Each time for three times he sucked, and spit something into his hand, and threw it in the fire. The last time he shouted, "I got it! I got it!"

The old man held out his hand and there, in the middle of his palm, was a pile of tangled black hairs, like a woman's hair combings. When Carrie saw the hair she knew what it was and how it had reached her boy.

"That old woman's a witch!" she screamed. "She poisoned the water, and my boy drank it. That's what she did, so her grandson could win the dance contest!"

"If that's so, and I have cured him," the Indian doctor assured

Carrie, "the old lady will die, so don't you worry about it. Just go on home."

They went home, Jimmy Bob walking as well as anyone on his healed leg. Four months later, at the winter powwow, they heard that the old Oto woman had died.

▼▼▼▼▼

Told to Alice Marriott and Carol K. Rachlin by several Indian inform-ants who prefer their names withheld. Tribal identifications and powwow locations have also been changed.

A World of Beauty:
The Peyote Religion

▼▼▼▼▼▼▼▼▼▼▼▼▼▼▼▼▼▼▼▼ COMANCHE AND KIOWA

The cactus plant peyote (Lophophora williamsii), *its component, mescaline, and the synthetic mescaline made in laboratories, LSD (lysergic acid), have come in for a large amount of journalistic attention in the mid-1960's. Little attention has been paid to the introduction of the peyote religion, known and chartered under the name of the Native American Church, to Indians north of Mexico. In the following story of the great Comanche chief Quanah Parker, who died in 1911, is the same blending of historical fact and myth-interpretation that there is in the story of Tsali.*

▼▼▼▼▼

Quanah's mother, Cynthia Anne Parker, was captured by the Comanches in Texas, when she was a little girl just ten years old. Her captors adopted her and were good to her. Cynthia learned to speak Comanche and almost forgot about English. She lived like a Comanche; she *was* a Comanche.

When Cynthia was a young lady, she fell in love, and married Nokoni, who was already famous as a chief of the Quahadie band. As a chief's wife, Cynthia was called on to be kind and good, to show the other women of her band a right example. She did all these things, and no Comanche woman was more respected than Nokoni's wife.

Cynthia had several children, but her favorite was her oldest son, Quanah, which means "the eagle." He grew up as a young man should, and except that his eyes were light, no one could have told him from a Comanche full-blood. He tended his parents' horse herds, he learned to break and train horses, and in time he went with war parties, raiding deep into Texas.

Those were the good years for the Comanches and Kiowas of the southern plains. The white men had come and built forts on the Indians' land a few years before, and the soldier chiefs had told the tribes they must lay down their weapons and learn to farm and live in villages, like Wichitas and Caddos. No Kiowa—no Comanche!—could live like that. They wasted a lot of valuable time that they could have used for hunting or fighting the Navahos and Utes, holding off the white soldiers.

But then the white men started a war of their own, off somewhere to the east, and the soldiers left the Comanche country. Then how they raided! No Texans and very few Kansans were really safe from the swooping down of the Comanches. The white people's stock was run away, their horses and women and children were captured, their men were killed, and their houses were burned. Truly, in those four years of the Civil War, the Comanches were the lords of the southern plains.

But then the white men came back, stronger than ever. They built a fort with stone walls near Medicine Water Creek, and moved in their men and horses. With them came a new kind of soldier, men with dark skins and hair so black and tightly curled that they looked like buffaloes. The Comanches called the blue-uniformed men with the gold X on their uniforms "the buffalo soldiers," and so the Tenth Cavalry was always known.

Between the buffalo soldiers, and the white hunters hired by the railroads, the buffalo were soon gone, and with them went the Comanches' way of living. Nokoni was dead in the fighting, and his young son called the Quahadies together.

"They are too strong for us," he said. "Let us take a share of land apiece to live on, and learn to raise cattle. Then we can sell the wo-haws [cattle] to the soldiers, and we can get rich from them, instead of letting the other white men take the money."

"We don't know how to farm," the other Comanches objected.

By this time Cynthia Anne had told her son the story of how she had been captured. He knew that he had relatives living in Texas.

"I will go and find my mother's people," Quanah said. "They can teach me how to raise stock, and then I can teach the rest of you."

Quanah traveled a long way and he looked for a long time, but he did finally find his mother's family. They were surprised to know that they had an Indian relative, and sent him back to bring his mother to visit them.

Cynthia Anne did not want to leave the Comanche country even though she was now a widow, and not a chief's wife. At last she agreed to go south with her son. Before she left, Cynthia looked all around her at the rolling red plains.

"Good-by, country of my heart," she said. "I know I will never come back." With her little daughter, Prairie Flower, clutched to her heart, Cynthia Anne left for Texas. She was right, for she died soon after she got there, and within a year Prairie Flower died too.

Now Quanah himself became sick; some people say with grief, and some people say with white man's tuberculosis. He had a great weeping sore on one leg. His grandmother, Cynthia Anne's mother, put poultices and dressings on it, and when that did no good she sent for a white man's doctor.

"Leave me alone," said Quanah, and turned his face to the wall. The metal springs creaked as he moved, and the sound seemed to stab at his wound. "If I had an Indian doctor, and could lie on the clean ground under an arbor, I might get better. Now I must die in a white man's bed. I am far from my people, but at least I am near my beloved lost ones. Leave me alone."

His grandparents went away and consulted with each other. The walls of the farmhouse were thin, and Quanah could understand what they said, for now he had learned some English.

"We can't get an Indian doctor for him," his grandfather said.

"No, they're too far away," the grandmother agreed.

"What are we going to do? We can't let him die," his grandfather insisted.

Suddenly Quanah heard his grandmother's voice grow lighter. "There's a Mexican woman in town, so I hear, who can do wonderful things," she said.

"A Mexican woman?" Quanah's grandfather repeated.

"A Mexican woman. What they call a *curandera* [healer]," the grandmother said.

"You wouldn't call in a *curandera*. You don't know what she might do."

"She's the next best thing to an Indian medicine man, and she's handy," said Quanah's grandmother, and she went out and saddled her own horse and rode into town. She returned with the *curandera* riding behind her on the saddle blanket.

When the two women went in to Quanah's room, he was still lying with his face to the wall, so still that they could not tell if he slept or was dead.

"He is Indian?" the *curandera* asked.

"Half Indian. He's my grandson," the old lady replied.

"Then he must be moved out of this house," ordered the Mexican woman. "Tell your husband to have the men build a shelter of branches, open to the north and south, so he will have the breeze, but be shaded. When he has been moved out there, I can treat him."

The men cut willow branches and bent them into a domed arbor, like the ones the Mexican Indians and the Comanches make.

"Where shall we lay him?" Quanah's grandmother asked.

"Put quilts on the ground and lay him on those," said the *curandera*. "Let him lie so that he can reach out and feel the grass with his fingers, with his head to the south."

And so they made Quanah's bed and so they laid him, only sure that he had not quite stopped breathing. There the *curandera* began her treatment, which lasted four days. Quanah himself remembered none of these things. Only on the morning of the fourth day he opened his eyes and saw the *curandera* kneeling beside him, with an earthenware bowl in her hands.

"Drink this," the woman said, raising Quanah's head and supporting it while she held the bowl to his lips.

The drink was as bitter as the death Quanah had been awaiting, but he swallowed it and lay back. As he drifted into sleep, forms and shadows of marvelous colors moved before his closing eyes. He felt the Mexican woman press something against his hand and close his fingers around it, and he fell asleep holding the token that she had given him.

When Quanah woke in the morning, he was wide awake. He reached out and felt the grass with one hand. The other was still clutched around the thing the Mexican woman had given him. He raised it to where he could see it, and saw a string of black beads, arranged in a curious pattern. From it there dangled a shorter string, and from its bottom bead a cross, with a man's figure on it. Quanah was still staring at the rosary when the Mexican woman came into the arbor and stood looking down at him.

"How are you this morning?" she asked.

"Much better," Quanah replied. Then he remembered. "What did you give me to drink yesterday?" he asked.

"That is a medicine of my people, the Yaquis," the woman informed him. "When you are better we will talk about it and I will teach you how it should be used."

It was eight days before Quanah could get up from his bed in the arbor, and stagger out in the sun. He sat on the ground and felt the strength of the sun and the earth fill his body. Presently the *curandera* came out of the house, where she had been helping his grandmother in the kitchen, and sat down beside him.

"Now I will tell you," she said. And she began, "Many years ago, my people were traveling from place to place to place. They went here and they went there, stopping only for a night anywhere, and going on again. They were hunting, the way your grandmother says your father's people used to. At last one woman was very tired. She was pregnant, and she lay down to rest. When she woke, her little son had been born.

"The woman was frightened. The village had gone on and left her. She and her new baby were all alone in the world. She didn't know what to do. She struggled to her feet and started on, in the direction she thought her people had taken.

"Soon the woman grew hungry. Her child was crying for food, but until she could eat and drink herself, she could not feed the baby. She sat down beside the trail and cried with fright and desperation.

"Then the woman heard a voice speak to her. 'Look beside you,' it said. 'Pick the plant that you will find growing at your left hand. It is food and drink for all the people. Take it with you, and when you find your people give it to them. Tell them to take it with prayer, and it will heal all their ills and sorrows.'

"The woman looked down, and there she saw a little round green cactus growing. She picked one button and scraped off the white downy fuzz that grew on it. Then she ate the cactus, and, although its taste was bitter, she felt herself growing stronger and stronger, her breasts filling with milk for the baby, and all her courage returning. When she had nursed the child, she gathered all she could carry of the green peyote cactus, and followed the trail of the village again. By nightfall, she came up with them."

"That is a wonderful story," Quanah said.

"Yes," the *curandera* went on, "it is a wonderful story, and it is a true story. They called her Morning Star Woman because she brought the people a new day. Now we have a ceremony to remember her, and we eat the cactus as a sacrament, because it is one of God's good gifts to man. We pray and sing when we eat it, as we do in the priest's church, and that is why I gave you the prayer beads. When you are better, I will take you to a ceremony, and you can learn everything. Then you can return to your own people, and teach them this way of living."

Quanah stayed all summer at his grandparents' home in Texas. In the fall, when he had his full strength back, he returned to the Comanches. He had learned everything the *curandera* and her people could teach him, and now he taught his own people: to be generous, to be kind, to live good, clean lives, and to let people see that their religion was a good one, because the people who followed it were good.

In time, the Comanches shared their religion with other Indian tribes—first the Kiowas, and then with still others. Today people who worship in the Native American Church try to live good lives, and to help and comfort their neighbors when they can.

▼▼▼▼▼

Story of Quanah's illness and recovery told to Alice Marriott and Carol K. Rachlin by Marie Cox, Quanah's granddaughter-in-law. Story of Morning Star Woman told to Alice Marriott by Frank Givens (Eagle Plume).

Bird of Power

Like everything else, the peyote religion has its good and its bad sides. The story of Quanah shows the good side. In the following story of an event that took place in the summer of 1966, we have a glittering example of the bad side, of an occasion when the Native American Church not only did not protect against evil, but actually seems to have been a medium for witchcraft.

In the intricate ritual symbolism of the Native American Church, birds have a place of particular importance. Like the incense smoke of the cedar fire in the ceremonial tipi, birds and their feathers are believed to carry man's prayers directly to God.

For that reason, members of the Native American Church bring feather fans—some beautifully beaded, and others plain—or handfuls of loose feathers into the tipi meeting with them. Birds that are believed to have particular power, and quick access to the ear of God, are the bald eagle, the prairie falcon and red-tailed hawks, the water turkey with its naturally crimped feathers, and the scissor-tailed flycatcher.

The two outer tail feathers of the last bird are a delicate rosy pink, with black tips. It takes twenty-four such feathers to make a fan—a lifetime of collecting now that the birds are protected by state and Federal game laws. But the result justifies the effort, for these birds and their feathers have the greatest supernatural power of all.

The scissortail shuns dwellings, and is most often seen on fence posts or telephone wires along the roadsides. At the approach of a human being the scissortail darts away, almost invisible in the speed of its flight.

This same darting swiftness enables the bird to attack and kill many creatures larger than the flies from which it takes its name. The scissor-tailed flycatcher is known as "wild and fierce," and prayer ascends on its feathers with the same strength and speed.

▼▼▼▼▼

Getting Helen into the hospital had not been easy. She was a big, hard woman and a stubborn one, and she did not want to go. In the second place, since she lived in the city and not on the lands allotted to her by the government, she was not qualified to enter a United States Public Health hospital. She ordered her four sons, each of whom had had a different father, to leave her at home to die.

But when the intervals of consciousness between convulsions grew shorter, when the flashes of consciousness grew fewer and fewer, Helen's sons decided to defy her, and to move her to the city hospital. They had never defied their mother before in their lives.

"Don't move me," she begged when John, the oldest son, told her what he and his brothers planned to do. "Let me stay at home. Get the peyote doctor for me. Only my own religion can make me well again."

"No," said John. "You need to be in the hospital. Let us take you there; they'll take care of you."

"I won't go! You don't dare to move me! Get me the peyote doctor or I'll put a curse on you—I'll curse you and your wife and children. None of you will ever know what peace is again. Get me the peyote doctor, or that's what I'll do!"

But she was unconscious again the next second, and the brothers, standing beside her bed, looked at each other questioningly.

"Perhaps we should do what she says," said John.

"No," said Dave, the second brother. "That's superstition, that talk about peyote and curses and witching. The one thing they tell us over and over again at Government school is that those old ways are gone. They don't mean anything any more. What counts is if you can fix a television set.''

''I'm afraid,'' said Chris, the youngest of the four. He was only twelve years old, and he began to whimper like a child. ''I'm afraid. Mother always did whatever she said she would. She told me once she'd hold my hand in the fire for stealing, and she did it.'' He held up his hand. It was still withered.

''Let's do what she says,'' Ernest, the third brother, said. ''I don't want to disobey her. She always makes us mind. You don't know what will happen if you don't obey her.''

John changed his mind suddenly. ''I'm the one she said she'd put the curse on,'' he said, ''me and my wife and children. The rest of you haven't any children or wives. I say we ought to put her in the station wagon now, while she doesn't know what's happening, and take her to the hospital.''

It took all four of them to lift Helen's limp body from the bed and lay it on the mattress on the floor of the station wagon. Ernest drove, and the other three sat beside their mother. On the trip Helen wakened, and when she realized where she was and where they were taking her, the three strong youngsters could hardly hold her in the car.

''Curse you!'' Helen screamed again and again. ''You'll be sorry for this! I'll make you sorry—I'll make you wish you'd done as I said.'' Then her voice died away into mumbling and she was quiet the rest of the way to the emergency door of the hospital.

Once she was at the hospital, Helen quieted down. Perhaps it was the shots the nurses gave her to ease her pain. Her mind cleared and she was rational again; she even thanked the nurses and doctors for taking care of her, and smiled forgiveness at her sons.

One of them was with her at all times. As Helen grew weaker, the nurses put a cot in the room, and let whichever brother was staying that night sleep in the room.

One morning Helen opened her eyes, and looked directly at Ernest. ''You thought you fooled me, that last night at home,'' she said. ''You thought I was sleeping and didn't know what you said. Maybe the things I believe in are superstition. Maybe all that counts is fixing television sets.'' Her voice grew stronger. ''Hear what I tell you,'' she went on. ''When I am dead, never use my tipi again. Give away all my ceremonial things—feathers and beads and the punk stick for lighting cigarettes when I pray—everything—to your uncle. And burn my tipi. You won't mind doing it. It's all just superstition to you. The old Indian ways don't mean anything as far as you're concerned. Do as I say. Don't disobey me again. Give everything, including my scissortail fan, to your uncle, and be sure you burn that tipi.''

That night Helen died. Her sons placed her gently in the car again, and took her home, so the women of the proper clan could prepare her for burial.

When the women were busy and the men had gathered in the yard of the house, Ernest went indoors, and when he came out he was carrying Helen's fans and beads. No other woman ever had a fan to use in ceremonies, but Helen made her own rules, and she had two. The boy held them out to his uncle. "Here," he said, "she wanted you to have these."

"Thank you," said the uncle, taking the fans, the beads, and the fire stick from his nephew. "What did she want us to do about her tipi?"

"She told me to burn that," Ernest replied. "She said no other woman should own it. A tipi always belongs to a woman."

"That's a good tipi," the uncle's wife objected. "It's a shame to burn it. I wouldn't mind having it myself."

"Leave it alone," said her husband. "She said she would burn it so no other woman should have it. People die the way they live. She would have burned it if she were living, and she will burn it now that she's dead."

But his wife didn't give up easily. She had her heart set on owning Helen's fine white canvas tipi, and that was that. She came from another tribe and she had different beliefs. In the end she had her way.

"We can use it for the funeral service," the uncle suggested. "After that we can decide what to do about it."

"She told me to burn it," Ernest insisted.

"We'll hold the funeral service in it and then we can make up our minds," his uncle repeated, and the other brothers agreed to the plan. At last Ernest gave up and went along with them. He didn't want any quarreling in the family.

It took all next day to send word to the other members of the Native American Church to come to the all-night funeral service and the feast that would follow it on the morning of the burial. Everybody came. Few people had really liked Helen, but in their own ways they had respected and feared her. They would not stay away from a ceremony given in her honor.

Some of the women brought food from home, and others cooked over an open fire west of the tipi. The men brought firewood and water, and everyone worked hard to do as much as he could in advance. Although they were cooking and working with food, nobody ate any. It is best always to go into the peyote tipi fasting.

Just at sunset, when the lower rim of the sun's disk touched the earth, the uncle gathered together a bag of peyote buttons, Helen's fans and his own, a water drum and tobacco and corn husks for rolling cigarettes. The other people formed a line behind him, and the priest led them four times around the outside of the tipi, east, south, west, north, and back to the east door again. Then everyone went inside the tipi and sat down. In the center of the floor was a moon-shaped altar of white sand, with the points of the crescent open to the east. On the center of the floor inside the arc of the altar, a small fire burned. The priest sat on the west, behind the altar, which he covered with a bright-colored silk handkerchief. From his pouch he took a large peyote button—a father peyote. He made three advances with the button before he laid it in the middle of the handkerchief.

There was silence for a moment, and then the night of singing prayers began. The doorman laid Helen's fire stick with its end in the fire, so the white ash wood would smolder slowly through the night. When anyone rolled a ceremonial cigarette, the doorman lighted it with the fire stick.

At midnight the priest went outside the tipi, and blew four blasts, one to each corner of the world, on an eagle wing-bone whistle. The doorman brought the midnight water into the tipi and took it first to the priest, who drank four sips from the bucket. From him the water bucket went around the north side of the circle, was returned to the west, and then went from hand to hand along the line of worshipers seated on the south side. The doorman carried the water out, and the ceremony resumed.

Morning brings new day and new life, and the morning water is brought into the peyote tipi by a woman. Helen's sister-in-law rose, and her daughter followed her out, for it was the young woman who would carry in the bucket. The morning star was rising in the east and the sky was at its darkest.

There was a whir of wings and moving air brushed their faces as a bird flew between them. "An owl?" the younger woman asked, her face paling.

"It couldn't be anything else at this hour," her mother answered. "Don't be afraid. You haven't done anything wrong. It won't hurt you."

"Aunt Helen's spirit——" the girl quavered.

"Aunt Helen wouldn't hurt you. You were always nice to her,

and she was nice to you. She could be mean; she was as wild as a scissortail. But she wouldn't hurt you.''

Together they went to the house—Helen's house. The girl dressed in her best clothes, and took a new bucket to carry the water. The east was whitening as they stepped outdoors, and the dawn wind ran along the grass and brushed their ankles.

"Look!" the girl cried.

A bird was flying around the tipi, up and down, as if it were seeking a way in. It was not an owl, or any kind of night bird. It was a scissor-tailed flycatcher, beating its head and wings against the canvas, flying at the smoke flaps of the tipi and then, driven back by the faint cedar smoke, striking against the tipi cover.

"That's Ernest's back; he's hitting Ernest's back!" the mother exclaimed. At that moment the first of the four blasts of the whistle cut their ears. The priest was calling the day into being. The girl picked up the water bucket and the two women returned to the tipi as the bird fled before the piercing sound.

Inside the tipi was peace. People were tired, and their faces wore the withdrawn look that comes from fasting and sleeplessness. They waited for the morning water, as the girl set the bucket in the curve of the altar and knelt behind it.

The priest smoked and prayed. As the first shaft of the rising sun penetrated the doorway behind the girl, her father bathed her in cedar smoke from the fire; hands to heart, feet to heart, head to heart. She was ceremonially clean now, and the worshipers, wearily passing the bucket from hand to hand, drank more deeply than they had at midnight.

Into the silence came again that whir of wings. The bird was almost inside the tipi; then the fire flared suddenly and the intensified heat drove him back. The women rose and left, and as they stood outside again the bird flew between them. This time it was the mother who cried out and drew back. The girl was simply too frightened to move.

"Helen's bird! She came for her tipi!" the woman cried.

"She was wild and strong. You know she was wild and strong," her daughter repeated numbly. They watched the bird's darting flight, and then turned and ran for the safety of the house.

Presently the other women joined them, and began the last preparations for the feast.

"Did you see it? Did you see the bird?" Helen's sister-in-law asked.

"It was perched on Ernest's shoulder, pecking at him, when I came out," one woman answered. "It flew away when it saw me, though."

"Ernest promised his mother he'd burn her tipi. She'd want to punish him."

"Maybe. I don't know." They all stopped talking and went on with the last-minute chores.

The men came out of the tipi at last, throwing its door flaps wide against the outside canvas. The doorman poured the last of the morning water and the contents of the water drum onto the fire, which hissed, spit, smoldered, and slowly blackened. They carried their fans, wrapped, under their arms. Quietly, without hurrying, they walked away from the tipi. Before he reached the house, Ernest's hand went up and he rubbed his shoulder.

"I don't know what's wrong with it," he said. "All night long I felt as if somebody was hitting me there."

The women exchanged glances, but none of them spoke.

Ernest slid his shirt down over his shoulder. "Look at my back," he said to his aunt.

She stooped over him and examined the black and blue patch that extended from his shoulder down his ribs. "It's bad," she said, and then screamed, "Look! Look at the bird!"

They all looked as the bird flew into the open tipi and out again. "Perhaps she's satisfied now," Helen's brother said. "Now she's seen we haven't hurt it any."

Nobody answered him. Nobody moved. They all watched the tipi, but apparently the bird was satisfied, for it was gone.

"Put the food on the tables," Helen's brother said. "We'll all feel better when we've had something to eat."

The women served the food, and the men filled their plates. At first eating was difficult, but presently they began to taste the food, and then to enjoy it. For a moment companionship wiped away fear and sorrow.

Then that peace, in its turn, was shattered. A bowl of chicken stew fell from the niece's hands, as she stared at the tipi. "Fire!" she shrieked. "Fire!"

By the time they reached the tipi, it was gone. Only a huddle of blazing tipi poles piled across the altar and the fireplace remained. The scissortail shot upward before their eyes, its prayers answered and its duty performed.

▼▼▼▼▼

Told to Alice Marriott and Carol K. Rachlin by informants who prefer their names withheld. Details of the peyote ceremony have been generalized.

Modoc basket bowl with rising-mountains design, probably made c. 1875. (*Florence Hollenback collection*)

Basket bowl with pine-tree design, from Washoe, Nevada, c. 1920. (*Florence Hollenback collection*)

Cherokee sun disc with hands pointing counterclockwise. (*Stovall University collection, University of Oklahoma*)

Zuñi prayer sticks, darts, and Spider Grandmother's web, probably c. 1920. The web was used as a target. (*American Museum of Natural History collection*)

Cheyenne old-style man's fan with thunderbird design on handle, c. 1870. Eagle feathers are tufted with red horse hair. (*Dr. Harry L. Deupree collection*)

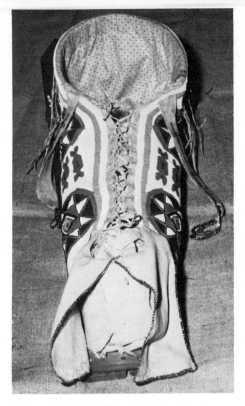

Kiowa child's full-beaded horseback cradle, made of buckskin on hand-hewn boards lined with trader's calico, c. 1910. (*Dr. Harry L. Deupree collection*)

Cheyenne tipi ornament, c. 1900.

Fox moccasins. (*Mary Neal, 1958*)

Fox ribbon appliqué skirt. (*Mary Neal, 1965*)

Fox ribbon appliqué skirt. (*Mary Neal, 1965*)

Part Four
THE WORLD WE GO TO

How Death Came Into the World

▼▼ K I O W A

There are the affairs of the world that was, the world that came into being with the creation. There are the affairs of the world that is—the world of the men and women who have become the heroes and heroines of legend, the world of the joking and experience of contemporary human beings.

And then there are the affairs of the afterlife—of the world that lies beyond what we call death, and of how that death came into existence.

Every North American Indian tribe has an explanation for the fact of death. Usually this is told as one of the "how and why" stories, but it is told in a serious mood, as a caution against questioning life and its problems.

These stories also explain the forms of certain animals. In the one that follows, the Kiowa Trickster-Hero Saynday, again in his heroic mood, tries to prevent death from coming into the world. The same story, with many variations, can be found from border to border and coast to coast.

▼▼▼▼▼▼

Saynday was coming along, and as he came he met the red ant. In those days the red ant was as round as a ball, like a lot of Kiowa women. It was a hot day. Saynday made himself small, no bigger than the ant, and they sat down in the shade of a prickly pear to talk.

"I've been thinking," Saynday said.

"What about?" asked the ant. Like most other people, she wanted to make sure what Saynday had on his mind before she said anything herself.

"Well, I've been thinking that some of the old people and animals in my world are beginning to die," answered Saynday. "It's too bad. Nobody should have to die. I believe I could work out a way so that they could come back to life after four days."

"Are you sure that's a good idea?" Ant asked.

"Why not?" inquired Saynday.

"Well, I think that if you keep bringing people back to life that way, over and over, the world will get too full. If you keep on bringing people and animals back to life, there won't be a place for anyone to go. I say that when people die, they should stay dead."

"I think you are wrong," Saynday argued.

"I think I'm right," Ant insisted. "The old people have lived their lives. They're tired. I don't believe they even want to go on living."

"But what about the young ones?" Saynday demanded. "If a boy gets killed in a hunting accident or on a war raid, or if a young woman dies in childbirth, shouldn't they have the right to come back and take up their lives? They've just begun to live."

Ant set her jaw stubbornly. "Saynday," she said, "you always want your own way. Now this time I think you're wrong. When people die, let them stay dead. Don't try to bring them back."

"If that's the way you want it, that's the way it shall be," Saynday replied. "If some day you regret your decision, remember it was yours. If you make your decision, you have to keep it. From now on, you will have to mourn like all other people."

"That's the way I want it," Ant insisted, and Saynday got up and went away and left her, sitting under the prickly pear.

Four days later, Saynday was coming back along the same track. Suddenly the air was filled with sorrow, with tiny sobs and wails. He made himself small again, and found himself sitting beside Ant, under the same prickly pear.

"What in the world is the matter?" Saynday asked.

"He's all dead," Ant sobbed. "A buffalo stepped on him and he's all dead. There wasn't enough left of him to scrape up. Oh, my poor boy!"

"I warned you," Saynday scolded her. "If you had let me have my way, I could have brought him back to life in four days. But no. You women are all the same. You know the best and you're bound to have your own way. If you hadn't been so stubborn yourself, your son wouldn't have had to die."

"Oh, my poor boy!" Ant wailed again, and she drew her butchering knife from its sheath at her belt. Before Saynday could move to stop her, she began cutting herself in two, just below the head.

"Now look here," Saynday scolded, grabbing the knife before she could cut her head completely off. "We've had enough dying around here for one day. Cutting yourself to pieces won't bring your son back; it will just make other people feel worse.

"Now listen to what I say: From now on, when Kiowa women mourn, they should cut themselves—their arms, their legs, their hair—even cut off a finger joint, because a woman brought death forever into the world. But no woman shall ever kill herself for sorrow."

And that's the way it was and that's the way it is, to this good day.

▼▼▼▼▼

Told to Alice Marriott by George Hunt, Kiowa.

How Death Came Into the World

MODOC

The following story is remarkably like the Kiowa version, considering the distance in space that separates the Modocs and the Kiowas. They have never heard of each other, in fact, except through wandering anthropologists and the news releases of the Bureau of Indian Affairs.

The Orpheus-Eurydice theme, is, however, unusual in North American Indian mythology.

Kumokums was living by himself near the Sprague River, and he began to get lonesome. He called all the animals together, to talk to them.

"Let's build a village here," said Kumokums, "where we can all live together."

The animals liked the idea of a village, but some of them didn't like the place. "It's too cold here, and the grass is stubbly," remarked the deer. "I think we should go to Yainax."

"I like cold weather," Bear informed them. "That's when I can curl up and sleep as much as I want to. I'd rather stay here."

So they discussed the matter, without ever really quarreling, and at last Kumokums got tired of all the talking.

"Listen to me," he said. "I called this council and I am its chief. We will have two villages. In the summer we will all live in Yainax and in the winter we will live here on Sprague River. Then everybody will be satisfied."

"How long is the summer and how long is the winter?" Porcupine asked.

"We ought to divide the year," Kumokums said. "Each can be six moons long."

"But there are thirteen moons in the year," Porcupine argued. "What are you going to do with the odd one?"

"We can cut it up," Kumokums decided, "and use one half in summer and one in winter, for moving."

Everybody agreed that that was a good plan, and they would go along with it. It was summer then and the middle of the Moon When the Loon Sings, so they all packed and moved to Yainax.

Kumokums and the animals lived very happily for many years, moving back and forth between their winter and summer villages. But they were so happy and well fed and contented that too many babies were beginning to be born. At last Porcupine took matters into his own hands, and went to talk to Kumokums about it.

"Kumokums," he said, "there are too many people around here. Our old people are dying off, and still there's too many people. We all know that when people die, they go to a land beyond, and if they have been good they are happy. Well, everybody in this village is well fed and contented, so they have been good. Why not let them go to the Land of the Dead, and they can be happy there?"

Kumokums sat and thought it over for a long time. Then he said, "I believe you are right. People should leave this earth forever when they die. The chief of the Land of the Dead is a good man, and they will be happy in his village."

"I'm glad you see it that way," said Porcupine, and waddled off.

Five days later, Kumokums came home from fishing up Sprague River, and he heard a sound of crying in his house. He threw down his catch, and rushed to the door in the roof of his house. He climbed down the pole ladder through the smoke hole. His daughter was lying on the ground and his wives were standing around, wringing their hands and crying.

"What has happened? What is the matter with her?" Kumokums cried. He loved his daughter very dearly.

"She has left us," his wives cried. "She has gone to the Land of the Dead."

"No! She can't do that!" Kumokums exclaimed, and he stroked his daughter's head, and called her name. "Come back to me," Kumokums begged. "Stay with us here in our villages."

Kumokums sent his wife through the village to bring in the most powerful medicine men. They sang and prayed over the girl's body, but no one could bring her back.

Finally, Porcupine came waddling backward down the pole ladder through the smoke hole.

"Kumokums," he said, "this is the way you said it should be. You were the one who set death in the world for everybody. Now you must suffer for it like everyone else."

"Is there no way to bring her back?" Kumokums pleaded.

"There is a way," said Porcupine, and Bear, who is as wise as Porcupine, nodded his head. "There is a way, but it is hard and it is dangerous. You yourself must go to the Land of the Dead, and ask its chief, who is your friend, to give you your daughter back."

"No matter how hard or how dangerous it is, I am willing to do it," Kumokums assured them. He lay down on the opposite side of the house, and sent his spirit out of his body, away and away to the Land of the Dead.

"What do you want and whom do you come for?" the chief asked. He was a skeleton, and all the people in his village were skeletons, too.

"I have come to take my daughter home," Kumokums answered. "I love her dearly, and I want her with me, but I do not see her here."

"She is here," replied the chief of the Land of the Dead. "I, too, love her. I have taken her into my own house to be my own daughter." He turned his head and called, "Come out, daughter," and a slim young girl's skeleton came out of the hole in the roof. "There she is," said the chief of the Land of the Dead. "Do you think you would know her now, or want her in your village the way she is?"

"However she is, she is my daughter and I want her," Kumokums said.

"You are a brave man," observed the chief of the Land of the Dead. "Nobody else who has ever come here has been able to say that. If I give her to you, and she returns to the Land of the Living, it will not be easy. You must do exactly what I tell you."

"I will do whatever you say," Kumokums vowed.

"Then listen to me carefully," said the chief of the Land of the Dead. "Take your daughter by the hand and lead her behind you. Walk as straight as you can to your own place. Four times you may press her hand, and it will be warmer and rounder. When you reach your own village, she will be herself again. But whatever you do, do—not—look—back. If you do, your daughter will return to me.''

''I will do as you say,'' Kumokums promised.

Kumokums held out his hand behind his back, and felt his daughter's finger bones take hold of it. Together they set out for their own village. Kumokums led the way. Once he stopped and pressed his daughter's hand. There was some flesh on it, and Kumokums' heart began to feel lighter than it had since his daughter died.

Four times Kumokums stopped and pressed his daughter's hand, and each time it was warmer and firmer and more alive in his own. Their own village was ahead of them. They were coming out of the Land of the Dead and into the Land of the Living. They were so close Kumokums decided they were safe now. He looked back at his daughter. A pile of bones lay on the ground for a moment, and then was gone. Kumokums opened his eyes in his own house.

''I told you it was hard and dangerous,'' Porcupine reminded him. ''Now there will always be death in the world.''

▼▼▼▼▼▼

Told to Alice Marriott by Mary Chiloquin, Modoc.

Over the Hill

In the old days, the Plains Indians, as far as we know, did not have a clearly defined concept of the afterworld. As the teller of the story that follows phrased it, "All that talk about the Great Spirit and Happy Hunting Ground is a cliché and they've worn it out. The old people didn't think like that." Here, in Arapaho terms, is a concept of life after death.

When people die, they must go over a hill. There is a dividing line between the world we live in and the world of those who have gone before us. That line is the crest of a hill. In the old days, when all the country was open, and the prairies rolled as far as anyone could see, there was just the line of rocks on the crest of the hill. Nowadays, when all the country is fenced, there is a line of barbed wire there to mark the boundary.

When someone is very sick, he may start climbing the hill. It is hard work, going up, especially if his loved ones are here and calling him back. But if he is very sick and is suffering a great deal he will go on, toiling to reach the top of the hill in spite of those who are calling him to bring him back.

If he reaches the top of the hill, he can look across to the other side. The downhill slope is easy, and the grass grows thickly all the way to the bottom. At the bottom is a river, and across the river is a big Indian camp. The children are playing, splashing and swimming in the river, and riding horseback. As soon as they see the sick person, they call to him, begging him to join them. "Come down, brother—uncle—father"—whatever relative he is. But if the people on the side of the living love him enough to hold him, he will stay with them. He will know all the people in the camp, and will love them all, but the living can hold him if they beg hard enough.

This can happen more than once in a man's life. It will happen to women, too. A man who dies fighting and a woman who dies in childbirth suffer the same fate. There is no difference in the afterlife of the good and the bad; all share the same world after death. It is the Arapaho way not to judge people. This happened to me twice, on Saipan in World War II, and again in Korea.

▼▼▼▼▼

Told to Alice Marriott and Carol K. Rachlin by Richard Pratt, Arapaho.

The World Beyond

*For non-Hopis to try to explain to other non-Hopis the permutations
and combinations of the Hopis' most intricate religion, ritual, and
symbolism, is almost hopeless. Few Hopis will discuss such matters;
those who do, do so in fear and trembling. They will only say that it is
"like them other Pueblos," and as a close friend in one of those other
Pueblos once said, "Oh, if only you were even a tiny bit Indian—Cherokee, even—I could tell you so many things!"*

*A case in point is the "kachina" or "kacina" or "katcina" con-
cept. A kachina may be one of the forces of nature: life, death, fire
flood, or famine. A kachina may be the spirit of a much-loved ancestor
who, as the Hopis say, has "passed beyond." A kachina may be
man dancing to impersonate one of these spirits. Or a kachina, as is
most frequently said, may be what the Hopis call a "kachin tihu"—a
doll carved and painted to represent a spirit. These dolls are given to
children as a combination toy-catechism book, with which they play
but from which they also learn the essentials of their religion.*

*What follows here is the very little that can be told to a "bahana"
—a white person—by a Hopi priest. It is a Hopi belief that for
every Hopi there is a good bahana and a bad bahana, and that at some*

time in his life he will meet each. To one he may tell what he is
allowed to say; from the other the things of his heart must be secret.

▼▼▼▼▼▼

The San Francisco Peaks stand north of Flagstaff, Arizona, and for
many centuries they have been the most sacred places known to the
Hopis, except parts of the Grand Canyon.

Within the San Francisco Peaks, the kachinas live. They have a
very beautiful world. The corn grows thickly every year; the squashes
and melons grow at every joint of the vines; nobody knows how many
different kinds of beans the kachinas have. There are lakes of water—there are springs, too, like those on the mesas—but there are
really lakes of water, where the cattails grow tall and sweet.

The hills are covered with all the plants the Hopis use: wild spin-
ach and wild potatoes for food, rabbit brush and yucca for baskets,
and all the plants the Hopis need to make dyes for their basketry.

Highest up of all grow the sacred trees, blue spruce and juniper
and mountain mahogany and piñon. The kachinas can go out whenever they like and gather everything they need for their ceremonies.

During the growing months, from February to July, the kachinas
live in the villages with the Hopis. Nobody can see them, except when
they come out of the kivas to dance in the plaza, but the Hopis know
the kachinas are there, and they feel that they and their crops are
safe.

Late in July, the kachinas go home to the San Francisco Peaks.
They dance for the people one last time, and give presents to all the
children. Then the kachinas go over the edge of the mesa, and you can
see the tall rain columns marching across the desert to the San Francisco Peaks.

Naturally, every Hopi wishes to join the spirits of his loved ones
who have passed beyond. To that end he keeps his heart pure and is
kind and generous to other people.

When a bad person—one who is known as ka-Hopi, or not Hopi—dies, his fate is very different. The Two Hearts, or witches, take
him by the hand as soon as the breath is out of his body, and they lead
him away to their own country. The country of the Two Hearts is as
bad as they are themselves. You may live in a village all your life with
a Two Heart, and the only way that you can tell he is a witch is that
the people in his family keep dying off. Every time a Two Heart
works his wickedness and hurts somebody else, he must give up one of
his own kinfolk.

The country of the Two Hearts is a desert. It is dry, dry, and it has no water holes. The ka-Hopi must crawl through it on his hands and knees; when he is too weak, he crawls on his belly. Sometimes the ka-Hopi has a vision of someone he loved and he begs and pleads for water, for shade, for rest. But no matter how much his loved one wants to help the ka-Hopi, he cannot do so.

That is what happens to Hopis who do wrong, and who are selfish and cruel. No Hopi wants to suffer that way.

There was a young couple who married, many years ago. Naturally, the husband went to live in his wife's mother's house. At first everything went very well, but then the husband began to feel nervous. He felt as if someone were looking at him all the time. He glanced here and there, over his shoulder, up at the sky, down at the earth, but he could see nobody.

They lived on the very top of the mesa, and down at its foot was the old cemetery. When people were wrapped in their blankets, their faces covered over with cloud cotton, and they were buried, their relatives smashed pottery bowls on their graves, and gave away everything the dead ones had owned. Nobody ever went near the cemetery at any other time, unless he took the burro trails from the spring that led past its outer edge. Only Two Hearts went there, to gather more power to hurt people.

Presently the young husband noticed that his wife's relatives were dying off. They were young people, hard workers, and lived good lives, but they would sicken and die, leaving their children to be taken care of by the women of the children's clans.

The young wife did not mourn aloud—that is not the Hopi way. But often in the night her husband woke to find his wife's body shaking with sobs, at his side. When the husband asked her what was wrong, the wife told him that she was crying because they had no children. That was true, although they loved each other very much, and wanted children, and tried to have them.

This went on for a long time—about four years. The husband grew more and more disturbed. Once he went back to his mother's house, in another village, but his wife followed him, crying and begging him to come home, so at last he gave up and went with her.

One night it was getting dark, and the wife said to her husband, "I wonder where my mother is? I don't think she should be out so late."

"I don't know where she's gone," the husband answered. "I've been in the fields all day. How would I know what you women are doing?"

"Well, I wish you'd go and look for her," his wife said.

"Not till I eat my dinner," the husband answered.

She gave him beans boiled with mutton, and some baked corn, and a cup of coffee. When he had finished he got up and said, "That was a good meal. I'll go and look for your mother now."

"All right," said his wife. "Will you take the water canteen with you and fill it at the spring? I'm almost out of water."

The husband grumbled a little, but he finally took the flat-sided canteen and slung it with a strap across his forehead, the way a woman would carry it. It was dark, and none of the other men would see him carrying water the way a woman would.

The young man climbed down the track toward the spring, feeling his way very carefully, because the pebbles were rough under his moccasins. He reached the spring safely, and held the canteen under its trickle until the jar was full. Then he slung it across his forehead and down his back, and started back toward the village to look for his wife's mother. He thought she might be visiting some relatives.

Just as he reached the edge of the old cemetery, something struck him in the back, and he felt legs locked around his hips.

"I'm going to take you," a voice hissed in his ear. The man couldn't tell if it was a man's or a woman's. "I'm going to take you right now, away from here. All of us Two Hearts are holding a meeting, and it's my turn to bring in a new member. I'm going to take you to the Two Heart kiva and make you one of us. If I don't, they'll kill me."

"You can't do that," the man answered. "I'm a kachina priest, and the kachinas will protect me."

"I'm going to ride you like a mule," the Two Heart hissed. It began beating him with a clump of yucca. "Do what I tell you and go where I tell you to go. I've captured you, and now you'll be one of us."

"The kachinas will protect me," the man insisted.

Again the Two Heart beat him with the yucca. "Do what I say," it insisted.

The man struggled again, and tried to throw the Two Heart off, but in vain. It only beat him more, and at last he gave up and followed its directions to the Two Heart kiva. In his heart he was praying to the kachinas, telling them he had tried to be a good man and take care of his family, that he was studying to be their priest, and that he believed that their power was stronger than that of the Two Hearts.

At last the wall of the mesa loomed in front of them. The Two

Heart slipped from the man's back, and knocked four times against the rock. It opened in front of them. Inside, the man saw many people he knew sitting in council. Outside, in the dim light from the fire in the kiva, when he turned his head, he saw his wife's mother. Between the man and his mother-in-law stood the Sun God kachina, the strongest of all the good kachinas.

"Go home to your wife," said the Sun God. "You will always be safe."

The husband, with his water canteen still on his back, went home. "I couldn't find your mother anywhere," was all that he said as he put it down.

They went to bed, then, and late at night they heard the door open and the old lady come in. She slipped into her own bed very quietly, but they knew she was there. The husband prayed to the kachinas all night; he dared not sleep with a Two Heart in the house.

From that day on, the old woman withered and shriveled. The younger members of the family grew round and strong and healthy again, but she wasted away. The only time she spoke she cried for water, but when they gave it to her she could not swallow it, not even when they tried to drop it into her mouth with a yucca blade. Within the year she died.

▼▼▼▼▼

Told to Alice Marriott and Carol K. Rachlin by informants who prefer their names withheld.

A Glass of Water, Please

SAUK

*Like many other North American Indian tribes, the Sauk have no
clearly formulated concept of an afterlife. Their expression in speak-
ong of a person who has died is, ''He went.''*

*It is clear that in Sauk belief the dead person's soul leaves his body
immediately with his breath. The physical body is returned to the
members of the person's own family, who, within four years, must
adopt another person of the same age and sex as a replacement for the
one who is gone. From that time on, the adopted member of the family
is addressed by kinship terms, and is treated entirely as his counterpart would have been.*

*While there is no clear definition of Heaven as such, it is clear that
unhappy souls—those of persons who have died dissatisfied, who have
done evil in their lifetime, or who have not been replaced by adop-
tion —return to earth, usually in the form of owls.*

*The owl is a bird of ill omen to every North American tribe, and is
either the harbinger of death or the bearer of a message from the dead.
An owl can cause facial paralysis if it is glimpsed at night. In this
story, the owl fulfills its threefold function: it warns, it demands, and
it punishes.*

Nina and Joe lived about a mile from Joe's father. The two houses had been built about the same time, and Joe worked both allotments, for his father was too old to do much physical labor.

There was a lot of visiting back and forth. The old man lived alone, so Joe's children went over to see their grandfather almost every day. In the evening, when their work was finished, Joe and Nina would go to the old man's house, usually taking some food with them. He could cook, but he didn't like to, so Nina saw to it that there was something in the house he could heat up the following day.

Joe and Nina never stayed out late because they didn't want the children to be alone in the house too long at a time. One evening, as they were walking up the lane, they heard a cry overhead, and an owl swooped past them diving through the trees in the direction of Joe's father's house.

"Something bad will happen!" Nina cried, drawing her shawl over her head.

"Maybe not," Joe shakily reassured her. "Maybe it will be all right."

"He went to your father's place! Something bad will happen to him!"

"Do you want to go back and see?"

"No, we'll go the first thing in the morning."

When they got over there the next day, the old man seemed to be all right at first. He was sitting in his chair by the table, with a cup of coffee in front of him. When he tried to lift the cup to his lips, though, he could not control his hands, and when he tried to stand up he could not move from his chair.

Nina and Joe put Joe's father to bed, and debated what was the best thing to do. Should they go for a doctor, or ask a neighbor to go? Should they send one of the children? They hardly knew and yet they had to make the decision. It was the old man who made up their minds for them. A strange, choking cry, like an owl's cry, came from his dry lips.

Nina hurried into the next room. "He wants water," she announced when she returned. She picked up a cup and spoon from the table. "Come with me," she ordered her husband, and Joe obediently followed his wife into the next room. He stood by his father's bedside while she let one drop of water at a time drip into the old man's mouth. He swallowed it, little by little, and when he was satisfied, Nina set down the cup and spoon on a chair.

"He needs water," she said. "We've got to keep giving him water." Day and night, for four days, she stayed with her father-in-

law, and whenever that choked, owl's cry came, Nina dripped water
into the old man's mouth. Joe came and went, for farm work waits for
neither life nor death, but at the end of the fourth day he could see
that his wife was worn out.

"Go on back home," he instructed her that evening. "Get some
rest. I'll stay with him during the night."

"Are you sure you can take care of him?"

"Sure I'm sure. I've watched you give him water about a hundred
times, I bet."

"All right," said Nina, reluctantly. "I'll go home now, and be
back in the morning." She wrapped her shawl around her and set
out. Somewhere in the grove of trees behind the house she thought she
heard an owl call, but she covered her ears in order not to hear
it.

It was not quite sunrise when Nina left her own house to go back
to her husband and his father. She had not slept well, probably because she was too tired. When she came in, the old man was choking
and strangling, and Joe was holding him up. Before she could reach
them, her father-in-law straightened and died.

"I tried to give him water the way you did," Joe exclaimed. "I
did the best I knew how. Sometimes I thought he swallowed it, and
then I'd find it spilled all over the pillow."

"Never mind now," Nina reassured him "We have to get word to
his family. He belongs to them, now. You belong to his clan and you
have to tell them."

That night the relatives sat up with the body. It sounded as if all
the owls in the country were in the grove, talking and arguing. Nobody dared go outside until it was broad daylight and the owls were
still.

When the funeral and the funeral feast were over, Joe and Nina
went home. They sent the children, who had been with them all day, to
bed, and presently they dropped down themselves, too tired to sit
up.

Then the owl—just one owl—called outside the bedroom window.

"He still wants water," Nina said. "Joe! Get up! Give him a
glass of water."

But Joe mumbled sleepily, and when she prodded him again shook
his head in refusal. "He's dead, isn't he?" he exclaimed. "How can
he want a glass of water now?"

"He came back for a drink," Nina insisted. "If you don't give it
to him, something bad will happen."

It became a point of argument between them; one of those mean-

ingless disputes that arise because people are overtired and go on
resisting each other as if they were fighting the whole world. On the
fourth night, Nina could stand it no longer. She herself got up out of
bed and set a glass of water on the back porch. The owl was still.

After breakfast, Joe got up and stretched. "I'll hitch up the
wagon and get in a load of firewood," he said. "We've almost used
up what we had, what with the feast, and my not having time to go
and get more."

"All right," Nina agreed. She herself felt more tired than ever,
drained and exhausted as she had not been before. The children had
gone off to school, and she forced herself up from the table and began
to gather the dishes and pile them by the sink. The sink window
overlooked the yard, and she watched Joe throw the harness over the
horses' backs, and lead them up to the wagon shafts. The horses
hadn't been worked all those days, and they were frisky. Joe got them
harnessed and was just swinging himself to the wagon seat when the
owl swooped across the yard.

The horses spooked. Joe was thrown between the shafts of the
wagon, and by the time the horses were stopped by the yard fence and
Nina reached him, he was hanging limply upside down by his broken
leg, unconscious.

"I told you," Nina muttered over and over as she worked to free
him. "I told you. I said something bad would happen if you didn't
set out the glass of water."

▼▼▼▼▼

Told to Carol K. Rachlin by Bertha Manitowa Dowd, Sauk.

The Womb of the Earth

To the Hopi, Spider Grandmother and the Twins, usually called the War Twins, rank with the other great supernaturals, and transcend even the kachina spirits. While kachinas may come and go—there is, for instance, a highly respected Mickey Mouse kachina who once brought rain when none of the older supernaturals were able to do so—Grandmother Spider and the Twin Grandsons remain immutable.

Grandmother Spider is described as "the little gray one, who always lives in corners of houses." For that reason, no good Hopi housewife ever destroys the spider or her web. If she must, a Hopi woman will lift the gray spider on her broom, and set the creature outdoors.

Grandmother Spider, the supernatural, is the representative of the feminine principle to the Hopi, as to many other North America Indian groups. She is Eve and Lilith combined; She is the guardian of our mother, the Earth, and is the spirit who can lead human beings back into the Earth's womb.

The Twins are one good and one bad, but they can act together for either good or evil, as the whim takes them. Generally, Older Brother represents the power of good; Younger Brother the power of evil. They are represented in rock paintings and carvings, and probably wood carvings of the Twins and their Grandmother have been made, but have not been seen knowingly by non-Hopi eyes.

205

This is not a story. It is a simple, direct statement of fact, delivered by a Hopi to a non-Hopi, as a warning against trespassing on sacred places, even by accident. But the end is in the beginning—Grandmother and the Twins are the guardians of life and death, and must be respected as such by everybody.

▼▼▼▼▼

Over on Third Mesa, the western mesa, there is a path down one side, from the village on the mesa top to the fields in the valley. Men use it to go to their farms and orchards, and women sometimes travel that path when they go from one mesa village to another.

Halfway along the path there is a spring. Whoever uses the path must lay a stick of firewood beside the spring as an offering, because that is where Grandmother Spider lives, under the rocks beside the water. Sometimes you can see her sitting there, a little old gray lady, spinning. She is always busy.

Whoever sees Grandmother Spider must hurry on, and not stop to speak to her. If he is going to his field, or on some other errand, he must just lay down his stick of firewood and pass on. That is, if he is a Hopi man or woman, who has been through the kachina initiation.

If a child who has not been initiated, or a non-Hopi, takes that path, he may be in great danger. The War Gods stand there at the head of the path. They can make themselves visible if they want to. Older Brother tries to warn the traveler away, but Younger Brother smiles at him sweetly, and tries to coax him to go along the path, down to Grandmother Spider's home.

Once the person who should not take that way has set his foot on it, he is helpless. He must go on. When he gets to the spring, Grandmother Spider is there waiting for him, smiling and beautiful and beckoning. And the person to whom she beckons cannot disobey her. He must follow her into her house, under the rock, into the womb of our mother, the Earth.

When you walk around Third Mesa, which is the only Hopi mesa where non-Hopis are permitted to live, you must be very careful. Do not take any path down the mesa side unless you see the children using it. If they are allowed to walk a path, it should be safe for anyone.

▼▼▼▼▼

Told to Alice Marriott by an unnamed Hopi informant.

BIBLIOGRAPHY

This is not a complete bibliography of North American Indian mythology. It is not a complete list of the many publications consulted by the compilers of this book. It is a gathering of comparative materials, for the most part, so that different versions of the same myth can be set side by side.

The encyclopedic works of Stephen Barrett and Stith Thompson are not listed. Obviously, no one could write anything about North American Indian mythology without familiarizing himself with these world-famous sources.

All these titles and many many others were consulted during the preparation of this book. As was stated in the introduction, the compilers' main purpose has been to rely on original field research for the versions used here.

Angulo, Jaime de. *Indian Tales.* New York: A. A. Wyn, Inc., 1953.

Bancroft, Hubert Howe. *The Native Races,* Vol. III, *Myths and Legends.* San Francisco: Bancroft, 1883.

Barbeau, Marius. *Indian Days on the Western Prairies.* National Museum of Canada, Bull. 163, Ottawa, 1960.

Benedict, Ruth. *Tales of Cochiti Indians.* Bureau of American Ethnology, Bull. 98, Washington, D.C., 1931.

—. *Zuñi Mythology.* Columbia University Contributions to Anthology, Vol. XXI, New York: Columbia University Press, 1935.

Brill, Charles, J. *Conquest of the Southern Plains.* Norman, Oklahoma: University of Oklahoma Press, 1938.

Brown, Joseph Epes. *The Sacred Pipe of the Oglala Sioux.* Norman, Oklahoma: University of Oklahoma Press, 1953.

Bunzel, Ruth L. *Zuñi Origin Myths.* Bureau of American Ethnology, Annual Report 47, Washington, D.C., 1929–30.

Catlin, George. *North American Indians.* London, 1851.

Clark, Cora, and Williams, Texa Bowen. *Pomo Indian Myths.* New York: Vantage Press, 1954.

Clark, Ella E. *Indian Legends from the Northern Rockies.* Norman, Oklahoma: University of Oklahoma Press, 1966.

Culin, Stewart. *Games of the North American Indians.* Bureau of American Ethnology, Annual Report 24, Washington, D.C., 1902–03.

Cushing, Frank Hamilton. *My Adventures in Zuñi.* Dallas: Peripatetic Press, 1941.

Custer, Elizabeth Bacon. *Following the Guidon.* Norman, Oklahoma: University of Oklahoma Press, 1966.

—. *Tenting on the Plains.* Norman, Oklahoma: University of Oklahoma Press, 1966.

Dorsey, George A. *The Cheyenne,* Pt. II, *The Sun Dance.* Chicago, 1905.

—. *Ponca Sun Dance.* Chicago, 1905.

Dutton, Bertha P. *Sun Father's Way.* Albuquerque: University of New Mexico Press, 1962.

Dyk, Walter. *Son of Old Man Hat.* New York: Harcourt, Brace & Co., 1938.

Eastman, Charles A. *Old Indian Days.* Boston: Little, Brown & Co., 1917.

Fewkes, Jesse Walter. *Hopi Kachinas.* Bureau of American Ethnology, Annual Report 21, Washington D.C., 1903.

—. *Tusyan Migration Traditions.* Bureau of American Ethnology, Annual Report 19, pt. 2, Washington, D.C., 1898.

Goldfrank, Esther S. *The Artist of "Isleta Paintings" in Pueblo Society.* Washington, D.C.: Smithsonian Institution, 1967.

—. ed. *Isleta Paintings.* Washington, D.C.: Smithsonian Institution, 1962.

Grinnell, George Bird. *By Cheyenne Campfires.* New Haven: Yale University Press, 1962.

—. *The Cheyenne Indians.* New York: Cooper Square Publishers, 1962.

—. *Fighting Cheyennes.* Norman, Oklahoma: University of Oklahoma Press, 1956.

Hagan, William. *Sauk and Fox Indians.* Norman, Oklahoma: University of Oklahoma Press, 1958.

Hammond, G. P. *Oñate and the Founding of New Mexico.* New Mexico Historical Review, Vol. I, 1962.

Harrington, J. P. *Ethnography of the Tewa Indians.* Bureau of American Ethnology, Annual Report 29, Washington, D.C., 1907–08.

Hodge, Frederic Webb, et al. *Handbook of American Indians North of Mexico.* Bureau of American Ethnology, Bull. 30, Washington, D.C., 1910.

International Journal of American Folklore. Philadelphia: American Folklore Society.

Jackson, Donald, ed. *Black Hawk: An Autobiography.* Urbana, Ill.: University of Illinois Press, 1955.

Jones, William. *Ethnography of the Fox Indians.* Edited by Margaret Welpley Fisher. Bureau of American Ethnology, Bull. 125, Washington, D.C., 1939.

Kilpatrick, Jack Frederick, and Kilpatrick, Anna Gritts. *Eastern Cherokee Folktales.* Bureau of American Ethnology, Bull. 196, pp. 385–447, Washington, D.C., 1966.

—. *Friends of Thunder.* Dallas: Southern Methodist University Press, 1964.

—. *Run Toward the Nightland.* Dallas: Southern Methodist University Press, 1967.

—. *The Shadow of Sequoyah.* Norman, Oklahoma: University of Oklahoma Press, 1965.

—. *The Wahnenauhi Manuscript: Historical Sketches of the Cherokees.* Bureau of American Ethnology, Bull. 196, pp. 179–213, Washington, D.C., 1966.

—. *Walk in Your Soul.* Dallas: Southern Methodist University Press, 1965.

LaBarre, Weston. *Peyote Cult.* New Haven: Yale University Press, 1939.

Link, Margaret Schevill. *The Pollen Path.* Palo Alto, California: Stanford University Press, 1956.

McKenney, Thomas L. and Hall, James. *History of the Indian Tribes of North America.* Edinburgh, 1933.

Marriott, Alice. *Greener Fields.* Chapter 8. Garden City, New York: Dolphin Books, Doubleday & Company, 1962 (paper cover).

—. *Maria: The Potter of San Ildefonso.* Norman Oklahoma: University of Oklahoma Press, 1948.

—. *Saynday's People.* Lincoln, Nebraska: University of Nebraska Press, 1963.

—. *Ten Grandmothers.* Norman, Oklahoma: University of Oklahoma Press, 1945.

—. Unpublished field notes on the Cheyenne, Hopi, Kiowa, and Tewa Indians.

—. *Winter-Telling Stories.* New York: Thomas Y. Crowell Company, 1947.

Mathews, John Joseph. *The Osages.* Norman, Oklahoma: University of Oklahoma Press, 1962.

Michelson, Truman. *Fox Miscellany.* Bureau of American Ethnology, Bull. 114, Washington, D.C., 1937.

—. *Notes on the Fox Wâpanōwiweni.* Bureau of American Ethnology, Bull. 105, Washington, D.C., 1932.

Mindeleff, Cosmos. *Navaho Houses.* Bureau of American Ethnology, Annual Report 17, pt. 2, Washington, D.C., 1896.

Mooney, James. *Myths of the Cherokees.* Bureau of American Ethnology, Annual Report 19, pt. 1, Washington, D.C., 1888.

Opler, Morris Edward. *Myths and Tales of the Chiricahua Apache Indians.* Memoirs of the American Folklore Society, Vol. XXXVII, Philadelphia, 1942.

Parsons, Elsie Clews. *Pueblo Indian Religion.* Chicago: University of Chicago Press, 1939.

Powell, Rev. Fr. Peter John. Unpublished Cheyenne Field Notes.

Rachlin, Carol K. *Native American Church in Oklahoma.* Chronicles of Oklahoma, Oklahoma Historical Society, Vol. XLII, No. 3, pp. 262–272, Oklahoma City, 1964.

—. *Tight Shoe Night.* Mid Continent American Studies Journal. Vol. 6, No. 2, pp. 84–100, 1965.

—. Unpublished field notes on the Sauk and Fox Indians.

Radin, Paul. *The Trickster: A Study in American Indian Mythology.* New York: Bell Publishing, Inc., 1956.

Ray, Verne F. *Primitive Pragmatists: The Modoc Indians of Northern California.* Seattle, Washington: University of Washington Press, 1963.

Reichard, Gladys A. *An Analysis of Coeur d'Alene Indian Myths.* Memoirs of the American Folklore Society, No. 41, Philadelphia, 1947.

Roediger, Virginia More. *Ceremonial Costumes of the Pueblo Indians.* Berkeley, California: University of California Press, 1961.

Simmons, Leo W. *Sun Chief: The Autobiography of a Hopi Indian.* New Haven: Yale University Press, 1942.

Smith, E. A. *Myths of the Iroquois.* Bureau of American Ethnology, Annual Report 2, Washington, D.C., 1881.

Swanton, John R. *Indians of Southeastern United States.* Bureau of American Ethnology, Bull. 137, Washington, D.C., 1946.

—. *Religious Beliefs and Medical Practices of the Creek Indians.* Bureau of American Ethnology, Annual Report 42, Washington, D.C., 1924–25.

Thomas, A. B. *After Coronado.* Norman, Oklahoma: University of Oklahoma Press, 1935.

—. *Forgotten Frontiers.* Norman, Oklahoma: University of Oklahoma Press, 1932.

Tilghman, Zoe A. *Quanah, the Eagle of the Comanches.* Oklahoma City, Oklahoma: Harlow Publishing Corp., 1938.

Underhill, Ruth. *The Navahos.* Norman, Oklahoma: University of Oklahoma Press, 1956.

Velarde, Pablita. *Old Father, the Story Teller.* Globe, Arizona: Dale Stuart King, 1960.

Waters, Frank. *Masked Gods: Navaho and Pueblo Ceremonialism.* Albuquerque: University of New Mexico Press, 1950.

Wheelwright, Mary C. *The Myths and Prayers of the Great Star Chant and the Myth of the Coyote Chant.* Santa Fe, New Mexico: Museum of Navaho Ceremonial Art, 1956.

Weltfish, Gene. *Lost Universe.* New York: Basic Books, 1965.

White, Elizabeth Q. *No Turning Back.* Albuquerque: University of New Mexico Press, 1964.

White, Leslie A. *The Pueblo of Sia, New Mexico.* Bureau of American Ethnology, Bull. 184, Washington, D.C., 1962.

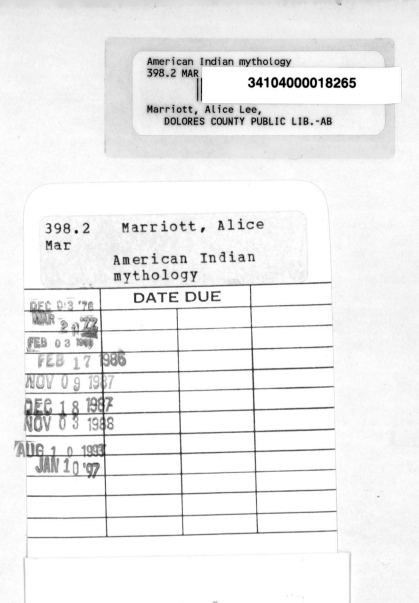